# Winning Your Benefit Appeal
# What you need to know

Child Poverty Action Group

Published by Child Poverty Action Group
94 White Lion Street
London N1 9PF
Tel: 020 7837 7979
staff@cpag.org.uk
www.cpag.org.uk
© Child Poverty Action Group 2013

A CIP record for this book is available from the British Library.
ISBN: 978 1 906076 77 1

Child Poverty Action Group is a charity registered in England and Wales (registration
number 294841) and in Scotland (registration number SC039339), and is a company
limited by guarantee, registered in England (registration number 1993854). VAT number:
690 808117

Cover and typography by Devious Designs
Content management system by KonnectSoft
Typeset by David Lewis XML Associates Ltd
Printed and bound in the UK by CPI Group (UK) Ltd, Croydon CR0 4YY

**Author**
**Simon Osborne** is a welfare rights worker at CPAG.

**Acknowledgements**
Many thanks are due to Jon Shaw from CPAG in Scotland and Judge Edward Jacobs for checking the text. Thanks to Nicola Johnston for her efficient and thorough editing and for managing the production. Thanks are also due to Katherine Dawson for producing the index and Kathleen Armstrong for proofreading the text. We are also particularly grateful for all the hard work done by Nigel Taylor of Devious Designs and Mike Hatt of DLXML.

## About Child Poverty Action Group

Child Poverty Action Group is a national charity working for the abolition of child poverty in the UK and for the improvement of the lives of low-income families.

To help achieve this goal, we have developed a high level of expertise in the welfare benefits system. We use this to support thousands of frontline advisers with our expert training and free helplines, enabling them to give families the best information and advice.

We also publish a widely used series of practitioner handbooks: our annual *Welfare Benefits and Tax Credits Handbook* (known as 'the adviser's bible') is used by Citizens Advice Bureaux, local authorities and law centres throughout the UK.

Our policy, campaigning and lobbying work builds support for policy improvements to help children living in poverty. We host the End Child Poverty campaign, a national coalition of charities, faith groups and other organisations working to hold the government to its target of beating child poverty by 2020.

If you would like to help with our campaign to end child poverty, please visit our website at www.cpag.org.uk. You can also get the latest news by following us on Facebook (www.facebook.com/cpaguk) and Twitter @CPAGUK.


### Keeping up to date

Advisers can get the latest information on appeals procedure and caselaw by booking on a CPAG training course. We can also provide your workplace with in-house training. See www.cpag.org.uk/training for more information.

Our *Welfare Benefits and Tax Credits Handbook* contains the latest information on universal credit, personal independence payment and other welfare reform measures. It also tells you all you need to know about entitlement to benefits and tax credits.

## Getting advice

Your local Citizens Advice Bureau or other advice centre can give you advice and support on benefits. See www.citizensadvice.org.uk if you live in England or Wales, or www.cas.org.uk if you live in Scotland.

CPAG has an advice line for advisers.

For advisers in England and Wales:
Telephone: 020 7833 4627, Monday to Friday 10am to 12pm and 2pm to 4pm

For advisers in Scotland:
Telephone: 0141 552 0552, Monday to Friday 10am to 12pm
Email: advice@cpagscotland.org.uk

# Contents

# Chapter 1
# **Introduction**

**This chapter covers:**

1. What is an appeal?

2. What does this guide cover and who is it for?

3. Which decisions have the right of appeal?

4. What does a representative do?

5. How do you win your appeal?

## What you need to know

- Appeals against benefit and tax credit decisions are made to an appeal tribunal called the First-tier Tribunal.

- Appeal tribunals are courts of law and must apply the law. However, they are not as formal as many courts and are not supposed to be intimidating. They are usually more concerned with establishing facts and considering evidence than with detailed disputes about the law.

- You do not need to be legally qualified or a legal expert to represent yourself or someone else in an appeal.

- It is strongly advisable to have a representative if you can.

- It is often worth appealing as there is a good success rate.

- Many decisions, especially those concerning illness or disability, are based on judgements or opinions which may be challenged in an appeal; however appeals can sometimes be avoided, especially where you can provide further information or evidence.

## 1. What is an appeal?

If you disagree about a decision about your benefit or tax credits claim, in most cases you can ask that it is changed. Usually, you must first ask for the decision to be looked at again by the 'decision maker'. If the decision maker looks at the decision again, if you are still unhappy then you can ask that an independent tribunal reconsider the decision. This is an appeal.

The tribunal that deals with benefit and tax credits appeals is called the 'First-tier Tribunal'. Appeals are possible against most decisions, including about whether you are entitled to the benefit or tax credit or not. A few decisions, mostly about how your benefit or tax credit is administered, cannot be appealed against.

Depending on the benefit or tax credit concerned, the decision maker will be an officer at the Department for Work and Pensions, HM Revenue and Customs or local authority.

The First-tier Tribunal can make any decision that the initial decision maker could have made. That means that the tribunal can 'allow' the appeal and make a different decision, or 'uphold' the original decision and confirm that it is correct. The tribunal's decision may be less favourable to you than the decision maker's. For example, it may increase the amount of the overpayment that you have to repay.

The tribunal must apply the law. It cannot make exceptions that the law does not allow. Winning your appeal means showing to the tribunal how the facts and evidence of your case mean that the relevant law, when properly applied, means that you are entitled to benefit.

### What is the tribunal like?

The members of the tribunal who decide you appeal are independent – they do not work for HM Courts and Tribunals Service (who administers your appeal) or for the organisation that made the benefit decision.

Tribunals are courts of law: they are independent, must apply the relevant law, and have a legally qualified judge. The tribunal asks questions and considers evidence, makes relevant findings of fact, and then applies the relevant law. The tribunal members know and have access to the relevant law.

However, appeal tribunals are more informal than most courts of law. The judge does not wear a judicial wig or gown, there is no dock or witness stand and other lawyers are not usually present. Oaths are not usually taken, although the tribunal may decide to require this in some cases. The tribunal is usually more concerned with establishing facts and considering evidence than detailed legal argument. Rather than having 'for' and 'against' cases, the tribunal hearing is more like a discussion – although the tribunal can ask questions and you may feel like the tribunal does not believe everything you are saying.

More information about HM Courts and Tribunals Service and the First-tier Tribunal is in Chapter 2.

## 2. What does this guide cover and who is it for?

This guide is about benefit and tax credits appeals to the First-tier Tribunal. It covers what you should do to ensure your appeal is successful, and looks at things like how to appeal, preparing for the appeal, gathering evidence and constructing arguments, writing a 'submission' and going to the appeal hearing.

It is also possible to appeal against a decision of the First-tier Tribunal. That appeal is made to a different tribunal, called the Upper Tribunal. Appeals to the Upper Tribunal are different in that they are much more concerned with the interpretation of the law. This guide is not about representing in appeals to the Upper Tribunal. However, some basic information about such appeals is in Chapter 7.

### Who is this guide for?

The guide is for anyone who wants to represent at an appeal tribunal. It is particularly for people with little or no experience of representing, although more experienced appeal representatives may also find it useful.

In this guide, the information and advice is addressed to 'you' as the claimant. If you have a representative, it is intended that the guide can also be used to aid her/his work on your appeal.

You do not have to have a representative and can represent yourself in your own appeal if you wish, or you can get help with it from a friend or relative. But it is always better to get help from a representative if you can.

**What CPAG says**

### Having a representative

It is strongly advisable to have a representative if you can, as s/he will provide a lot of help in preparing your appeal and increase the chances of winning your appeal.

A good representative is likely to have access to information and resources to help with the appeal, and may have some useful experience in representing in other cases. S/he is able to liaise with the various official bodies that are involved in your appeal, and may be able to get evidence for you and write a submission to send in to the tribunal.

## 3. Which decisions have the right of appeal?

Appeals can be made about decisions on entitlement to most social security benefits, including:

- employment and support allowance (including the work capability assessment)
- jobseeker's allowance (including things like if you are sanctioned for not taking part in an interview or not seeking work)
- personal independence payment and disability living allowance (including the disability tests)
- universal credit
- housing benefit, paid by your local authority
- child tax credit and working tax credit, paid by HM Revenue and Customs
- the 'habitual residence' and the 'right to reside' tests

## What the law says

### Mandatory reconsideration

If the decision is about:
- personal independence payment
- universal credit
- other benefits paid by the Department for Work and Pensions if it was made on or after 28 October 2013,

before you can appeal the decision maker must usually have looked at the decision again (carried out a 'mandatory reconsideration' of the decision) and issued you with the result of that in a 'mandatory reconsideration notice'. The letter from the decision maker about benefit entitlement must state whether there is a right of appeal or not.

*Section 12(3A)–(3B) Social Security Act 1998; regulation 7(2) The Universal Credit, Personal Independence Payment, Jobseeker's Allowance and Employment and Support Allowance (Decisions and Appeals) Regulations 2013; regulation 3ZA The Social Security and Child Support (Decisions and Appeals) Regulations 1999*

The requirement for a mandatory reconsideration before you can appeal does not apply to housing benefit. It is expected to apply to tax credits and other benefits paid by HM Revenue and Customs from April 2014. More information about mandatory reconsiderations is in Chapter 3.

A few decisions do not have the right of appeal. In particular, decisions about things like how and when a benefit or tax credit is paid do not have the right of appeal.

### What are most appeals about?

Currently, over three-quarters of benefit appeals are about illness or disability. Around 70 per cent of appeals are about employment and support allowance, mostly whether someone passes or fails the work capability assessment. Twelve per cent of appeals are about disability living allowance or attendance allowance, often about whether someone needs enough help with care or mobility to qualify. These figures may change over time, especially as personal independence payment replaces disability living allowance and as universal credit is introduced, although the work capability assessment is also part of universal credit.

Many of the examples and case studies used in this guide are about employment and support allowance (in particular the work capability assessment) and disability living allowance/personal independence payment. Although appeals about illness and disability benefits are essentially similar to other benefit appeals, they also involve some particular issues about the tests that decide whether or not you qualify, and medical evidence. Chapter 5 has information about some issues which often come up in those appeals.

## 4. What does a representative do?

The role of an appeal 'representative' is to put your case to the tribunal, or to help you to do so.

Representatives do not need to be a lawyer, or hold a legal or any other qualification, but the tribunal will expect that s/he:

- knows the case and the points s/he wishes to make
- helps establish the facts
- has a basic idea of the law relevant to the appeal

Representing someone at an appeal means more than just being there for reassurance or emotional support (valuable though those things are). Representatives may have access to personal information about the person who they are representing. Preparing the appeal ideally involves getting information from people such as doctors or employers, and accessing information about the benefit rules. It may involve researching the law.

Representatives need to present your case to the tribunal in the most effective way. So a good representative will help prepare your appeal by helping to gather relevant facts and evidence, checking the law and helping prepare for the hearing. In practice, tribunals very often like your representative to provide a written summary of your case (called a written 'submission') sent in advance of the tribunal hearing. The tribunal will expect a representative to cooperate with it in holding an efficient and fair hearing.

More information about the role of the representative is in Chapter 4.

If you do not have a representative, the tribunal does not expect you to do the job of an appeal representative. Instead it will ask you about basic facts in your case such as your medical condition and what happened at your medical assessment.

Box A
**Where can I find a representative?**

In practice, most representatives are not lawyers or legally qualified. They are often people working (either as paid worker or as a volunteer) for an advice centre, local authority, support group or charity. Ideally, a representative has some knowledge or training about the benefits system and appeals, but that is not always essential. Representatives are often working in:

- Citizens Advice Bureaux
- law centres (or a firm of solicitors doing social security work)
- local authority welfare rights units
- local disability charities or support groups
- unemployed workers' centres or trade unions
- hospitals and social work departments

## 5. How do you win your appeal?

### Is it worth appealing?

It is often worth appealing. Success rates are good, although they vary depending on the benefit concerned, whether there is an oral hearing of the appeal and whether you are represented.

There is no point appealing against a decision that is clearly correct under the law, as this cannot be changed by the tribunal. For example, sometimes you may be disappointed by the level of benefit rates that decide how much you are paid; but if the benefit award has been calculated correctly, then the tribunal is bound by the law setting the benefit rates and cannot change the decision. However, many decisions are matters of judgement or opinion, and another view of the same facts and evidence could be made. Sometimes, things simply go wrong.

Box B
**Common issues where an appeal may be necessary**

- Decisions about the work capability assessment for employment and support allowance and universal credit. The official medical report may be inaccurate, or the decision maker may have ignored other evidence or failed to seek evidence from someone who knows you.

- Decisions about the disability tests for personal independence payment, disability living allowance or attendance allowance. The official medical reports may be inaccurate, or the decision maker may have ignored other evidence or failed to seek evidence from someone who knows you.

- Many other decisions involving the exercise of judgement by the decision maker, such as whether you are living together with another person as part of a couple, whether you deliberately got rid of money in order to get benefit, or whether you have established and retained a 'right to reside'.

- In a few cases, there may be a complex issue of law involved, in which case you may be able to argue that the decision maker has misunderstood or misapplied the relevant law.

However, sometimes an appeal may be avoided.

## What CPAG says

### Successful appeals

The overall appeal success rate for all benefits and tax credits in 2012/13 was 38 per cent. This varies according to what benefit is involved: for example, the overall success rate for employment and support allowance appeals was 43 per cent. Where claimants attended their appeal hearing (ie, had an 'oral hearing' of the appeal) success rates were higher, at 47 per cent overall. Success rates were higher still where a representative helped with the appeal (63 per cent overall). Many appeal representatives report success rates at oral hearings of 70 per cent or more.

To increase your chance of success:
- ask for an oral hearing of your appeal which you attend so that the tribunal can ask you questions, clarify facts and discuss the evidence
- have a representative, if possible, to help with things like checking the law, gathering evidence and writing a submission, and assist you and the tribunal at the hearing
- be well prepared – understand what the tribunal is like, what the tribunal can do, and that the tribunal will ask you questions during an oral hearing

## Can the appeal be avoided?

An appeal is often necessary to correct an inaccurate or poor decision, such as one based on an inaccurate medical assessment, or drawing the wrong conclusion from the facts. That decisions are sometimes wrong is borne out by the high success rate on appeal.

However, as appeals are time-consuming for everyone involved and can be stressful, you should consider whether an appeal can be avoided – see Box C. The most common way an appeal can be avoided is to make the decision maker aware of information or evidence that s/he did not use when making the original decision. This could be, for example, a correction to something that was misunderstood in the medical, supportive medical evidence from your GP, or evidence showing that your income is different from that used by the decision maker. Decision makers are trained to be prepared to consider such information or evidence even after they have made their decision, and change it if appropriate.

If you must have a 'mandatory reconsideration' (see page 32) before you have the right to appeal, the process of having the decision looked at again provides an opportunity to send in further information or evidence. If the information or evidence becomes available after the sending of the mandatory reconsideration notice, it can still be sent in after the appeal has been made.

## Box C
### Avoiding an appeal

- Is the decision wrong or can you at least argue that it is wrong – for example, is it based on a judgement that could be challenged? Is it based on facts which have been misunderstood? If the decision is clearly correct, the tribunal cannot change it.

- Is there an obvious simple mistake in the decision that can be pointed out to the decision maker, which means that it clearly should be changed without the need for an appeal?

- Is there any further information or evidence, for example from a doctor or carer, that might persuade the decision maker to change the decision without the need for an appeal?

- If you must have a 'mandatory reconsideration' before you have the right of appeal, is there further information or evidence that could be sent in with that request for the decision to be looked at again, so that the decision is changed without the need for an appeal?

# Chapter 2
# The appeals system

## What you need to know

- Appeals are administered by a government body that is separate from the body that made the initial benefit decision, and has independent people making the decision.

- The people you deal with in the appeal are a tribunal clerk and the tribunal itself, which consists of at least a legally qualified judge, but could include up to three members.

- The tribunal reconsiders the decision under appeal, so it can uphold it or change it, including making an even less favourable decision. It does not have powers to award costs or compensation.

- Large numbers of appeals are received and dealt with every year, and the waiting time from start to finish is likely to be several months.

- The tribunal is usually held in a tribunal venue in a town or city near to you – for example, at a civic centre.

# 1. Who deals with your appeal?

Appeals are administered by an organisation called Her Majesty's Courts and Tribunals Service. The tribunal itself is called the First-tier Tribunal. It is independent and has between one and three members. It is assisted with administration by a clerk.

## What is Her Majesty's Courts and Tribunals Service?

The appeals system overall is administered by Her Majesty's Courts and Tribunals Service (referred to in this guide as HM Courts and Tribunals Service, but sometimes referred to as HMCTS). It is an agency of the Ministry of Justice and so it is a government body. However, it is independent of the organisations that make the initial decisions on your benefit and tax credits, such as the Department of Work and Pensions (DWP) or HM Revenue and Customs. The people that sit on the tribunals and make the decisions are completely independent of all government departments. HM Courts and Tribunals Service is responsible for the administration of a number of courts and appeal tribunals in Great Britain, not just the ones that deal with benefit and tax credit appeals.

## What does the tribunal clerk do?

The clerk deals with the administration of your appeal. The clerk, for example, sends out the papers relating to the appeal, sets the date for the hearing, and assists the tribunal with administration on the day of the hearing. In practice, you (or your representative if you have one) deal with the clerk quite a lot before the appeal hearing, and it is important to have a good working relationship with her/him.

## What does the First-tier Tribunal do?

The First-tier Tribunal considers appeals against decisions by:

- the DWP for benefits such as employment and support allowance, personal independence payment, disability living allowance, jobseeker's allowance and universal credit

- HM Revenue and Customs for child benefit, guardian's allowance and tax credits
- local authorities for housing benefit

For administrative purposes, the First-tier Tribunal is organised into a number of different 'chambers', which have different membership and sometimes slightly different rules, to hear different sorts of appeals. Social security and tax credit appeals are always included in the 'Social Entitlement Chamber' of the First-tier Tribunal. If you come across a reference to the Social Entitlement Chamber, that is simply a reference to the type of tribunal that considers social security and tax credit appeals.

## 2. Who is on the tribunal?

*What the law says*

### Members of the tribunal

The tribunal is made up of one, two or three members, depending on the type of appeal. There is *always* at least a legally qualified member, called the 'judge'.

Depending on the type of appeal, there may also be: a medically qualified member and a disability qualified member.

*Practice Statement of the Senior President of Tribunals, 'Composition of tribunals in social security and child support cases in the social entitlement chamber on or after 1 August 2013'*

### The judge

The judge of the tribunal must be legally qualified. Usually this means that s/he is a solicitor or barrister with at least five years' experience. S/he knows about the law relevant to your appeal. However, it is not a requirement that the judge has worked in social security – for example, s/he may have worked as a solicitor in family or criminal law.

The judge chairs the hearing as well as providing the legal expertise for the tribunal.

### The medically qualified member

This member of the tribunal must be a registered medical practitioner. Usually s/he is a doctor, such as a GP, but does not have to have specialist knowledge in the area relevant to your appeal. S/he is not required to have a legal qualification. S/he may also carry out medical examinations for the DWP's medical service (currently contracted out to a private organisation, Atos) but s/he will not have previously been involved in the decision you are appealing.

The medically qualified member provides the medical expertise for the tribunal. Except in industrial injuries disablement benefit cases, there is no actual medical examination at the tribunal.

### The disability qualified member

This member of the tribunal must be experienced in dealing with disability. This may be through having a disability her/himself or working with people with disabilities (in a professional or voluntary capacity) or being a carer. Someone who qualifies through working with people with disabilities could, for example, be a physiotherapist, occupational therapist or a social worker, but cannot be a doctor. Disability qualified members are not required to hold a legal qualification.

The disability qualified member provides experience and expertise about the effects of disability.

### Who sits on the tribunal?

The rules on tribunal composition are fixed in law, and you cannot ask for a differently composed tribunal.

*What the law says* ~~~~~~~~~~~~~~~~~~~~~~~~~~~~~~~~~~~~~~~~~~~~~

### Tribunal composition

A **three-person** tribunal consisting of a judge, a medically qualified member and a disability qualified member hears appeals about:
- disability living allowance
- personal independence payment
- attendance allowance

A **two-person** tribunal, consisting of a judge and a medically qualified member hears appeals about:
- the work capability assessment for employment and support allowance or universal credit
- industrial injuries disablement benefit (unless just about a declaration of an industrial accident)

A **judge sitting alone** hears all other appeals.

*Practice Statement of the Senior President of Tribunals, 'Composition of tribunals in social security and child support cases in the social entitlement chamber on or after 1 August 2013'*

There are some exceptions.

- If the case is only dealing with a question about the law and the doctor and disability tribunal members are not necessary, a judge alone may hear the appeal alone.

- There can be a second doctor if complex medical issues are involved, in particular in an industrial injuries disablement benefit case.

- If there are financial accounts to be examined, an accountant may sit with the judge to hear the appeal.

- If the case involves complex medical issues but is not about a benefit that requires a two- or three-person panel (for instance, a tax credit disability issue), the tribunal could also include a doctor. This is unusual.

- A tribunal can go ahead in the absence of one or more of the members usually required but there must always be at least a judge present.

### Typical tribunal compositions

| Benefit | Tribunal members |
| --- | --- |
| Disability living allowance/personal independence payment | judge, medically qualified member and disability qualified member |
| Employment and support allowance (usually involving the work capability assessment) | judge and medically qualified member |
| Housing benefit | judge |
| Jobseeker's allowance | judge |
| Universal credit | depends on the issue – usually a judge, but if it is about a work capability assessment it is a judge and medically qualified member |

## EXAMPLES

### Tribunals where there is more than one appeal

Joan has appealed against a decision refusing her personal independence payment, and also against a separate decision about whether she should be disqualified from receiving contributon-based jobseeker's allowance for a time for leaving her job without just cause.

Both appeals are considered by the First-tier Tribunal. But the actual tribunals that consider them must be different: a three-person tribunal for the personal independence payment appeal, and a judge sitting alone for the jobseeker's allowance appeal. In practice, it may be that both appeals are considered during the same tribunal session, but they will be heard separately.

Ron has appealed against a decision refusing him personal independence payment, and also against a decision refusing him employment and support allowance because he fails the work capability assessment.

Both appeals are considered by the First-tier Tribunal. Even though there may be some overlap in the issues in the appeals (because they both concern how Ron's illness affects him), the actual tribunals that consider them must be different: a three-person tribunal for the personal independence payment appeal, and a two-person tribunal for the employment and support allowance appeal. The tribunals must be completely separate – they must be on different sessions and by tribunals with completely different people on them.

## 3. What can the First-tier Tribunal do?

The First-tier Tribunal has the power either to confirm ('uphold') or to change the decision under appeal.

Upholding the decision means that the decision is not changed. If the tribunal changes the decision so as to give what you have asked for, this is sometimes called 'allowing' your appeal.

Changing the decision means that the tribunal substitutes the decision under appeal with one it considers to be correct. However, it does not have to make exactly the decision that you have asked for. For example, it may change your personal independence payment decision so as to give you the daily living component at the rate you asked for, but not the mobility component. This is sometimes called allowing your appeal 'in part'. In less common cases, the tribunal may change the decision under appeal, but make a decision which is actually even less favourable to you than the one you appealed against.

In essence, the tribunal can make or remake whatever decision could have been made by the decision maker. Sometimes this is described as 'standing in the decision maker's shoes'. It is a helpful image, as it gets across the point that the tribunal is reconsidering the decision that is under appeal – nothing more and nothing less.

**EXAMPLES**

### Allowing an appeal

Seren appeals against the decision that she has failed the work capability assessment. The tribunal considers that she has scored enough points to pass the assessment and changes the decision (allows her appeal).

### Allowing an appeal in part

Heidi appeals against the decision not to award her personal independence payment. The tribunal decides to change the decision under appeal so as to make an award of personal independence payment. However, the tribunal makes the award at a lower rate than Heidi asked for (it allows her appeal in part).

Ian appeals against the decision that he failed the work capability assessment, and so is not entitled to employment and support allowance. He argues that, firstly, he passes the work capability assessment, and so is entitled to employment and support allowance and, secondly, that as part of the assessment he should be placed in the support group.

The tribunal allows Ian's appeal in part. It holds that he does satisfy the work capability assessment (and so is entitled to employment and support allowance); but it does not hold that he is in the support group, and so he is placed in the work-related activity group.

### Can the tribunal make a less favourable decision?

The tribunal can make a decision which is even less favourable to you than the one you appealed against. This is because the tribunal can make whatever decision could have been made by the decision maker.

For example, you may have appealed against the refusal of the daily living component of personal independence payment, but do not want the tribunal to change the award that has been made for the mobility component, as you are happy with that. However, as it is the decision about personal independence payment that is under appeal, and the decision maker could allow or refuse either or *both* components, the tribunal has the power not only to refuse the appeal about the part of the decision about the care component, but also to remove the award of the mobility component, a part of the decision that you did not want altered.

This is relatively uncommon but sometimes happens in illness and disability-related appeals. See Chapter 5 for more information.

**Can the tribunal award compensation or costs?**

The tribunal cannot award compensation or costs. The tribunal has no power to alter the law: it has to apply the law as it stands. Because it is applying the social security or tax credit law, the tribunal has no power to make decisions about complaints about administration, or to award compensation.

**EXAMPLE**

**What the tribunal can and cannot do**

Danny was refused employment and support allowance because he was considered to have failed the work capability assessment. He appealed against the decision as he thought he should pass the assessment on the basis of scoring enough points for his mobility problems. At the hearing, Danny also tells the tribunal about what he felt was rude and unhelpful questioning at the medical for the work capability assessment, and for a finding that he should be paid compensation for his upset and inconvenience.

The tribunal allows Danny's appeal, because it considers that he scores enough points to satisfy the work capability assessment. So he is entitled to employment and support allowance. However, the tribunal cannot award compensation for his experience at the medical – that was not part of the decision under appeal, and so it has no power to make any awards for compensation.

The tribunal cannot award costs or damages against anyone involved in the appeal. So, for example, the tribunal cannot order compensation for you, but neither can it award costs against anyone, including your or your representative.

## 4. How long will the appeal process take?

Statistics from the Ministry of Justice show that around 507,000 social security appeals are received a year, and around 374,000 of them go on to be dealt with at tribunal. Over three-quarters of those concern employment and support allowance (the majority of appeals) or disability living allowance/attendance allowance.

### Clearance times

The amount of time it takes from receipt of an appeal at HM Courts and Tribunals Service to the point at which you are notified of the outcome is known as the 'clearance time'. The Ministry of Justice measures clearance times.

Box A
**Clearance times**

In 2012/13, 75 per cent of appeals were dealt with in 23 weeks or less, with the average time being 18 weeks. But there was some variation between different benefits and in particular between tribunals that consisted of just a judge sitting alone (eg, a jobseeker's allowance appeal) and one that also had other members (eg, an employment and support allowance appeal). The average clearance time for a jobseeker's allowance appeal was 15 weeks, that for an employment and support allowance appeal was 17 weeks, and that for a disability living allowance appeal was 22 weeks. There is some further variation in waiting times between different parts of the country. If you have a representative, s/he may have experience of waiting times in your area and be able to advise you of how long you are likely to have to wait.

*What CPAG says*

**Waiting for your appeal**

Statistics show that you can expect to wait at least several weeks, probably several months, for your appeal to be decided.

This waiting time can be very difficult, as you are likely to be in financial need and your circumstances may change (for instance, your health may worsen or improve) while you are waiting for your appeal. Get advice about any benefits you may be entitled to while you are waiting for your appeal to be dealt with.

You (or your representative) can ask the tribunal clerk to try to ensure that your appeal is heard as early as possible – sometimes this is called 'expediting' the appeal. It is best to provide particular reasons why in your case the appeal needs to be heard as early as possible (for example, because of a threat to your health or if you may be evicted).

## 5. Where will the tribunal take place?

There is no specific rule about where a tribunal must be held. There are tribunal venues in many towns and cities. Some are purpose-built, but many are in places like civic centres. The venue should be suitable for use by people with disabilities. When you are notified of the date of your appeal hearing, the letter includes details of the venue location and how to get there.

At the tribunal venue, there is usually a waiting room and a separate room in which the appeal hearing takes place. If you are anxious in the waiting room, you can ask if there is a private room available to wait in, although this is not available at all venues.

If you have any particular needs at the venue, for instance for a hearing loop or because of mobility problems, tell the clerk. S/he will make sure that you can access and use the venue.

See Chapter 6 for more about the appeal hearing and the layout of the room.

## What if you cannot make it to the venue?

In very exceptional cases, if you are completely unable to attend the tribunal venue at any time, the tribunal can take place away from a tribunal venue, such as in your home. Such a hearing is called a 'domiciliary hearing'. A domiciliary hearing can be requested, and the request must be properly considered. If the tribunal does not consider your request, or does not explain why it has refused the request, it may have made an error of law.

But there is no straightforward right to a domiciliary hearing, and in practice HM Courts and Tribunals Service will almost always want to allow the hearing to take place in a tribunal venue. If you wish to have a domiciliary hearing, you (or someone authorised to act for you) should write to the clerk and include medical evidence (such as a letter from a doctor) showing why that is necessary.

*What the law says*

### Domiciliary hearings

A request for a domiciliary hearing must be properly considered, and the decision explained, in order to comply with the right to a fair trial under Article 6 of the European Convention on Human Rights.

*CSIB/2751/2002 (decision of a Social Security and Child Support Commissioner)*

### Further information

There is a tribunal 'venue finder' at www.justice.gov.uk/tribunals/sscs/venues.

# Chapter 3
# Making an appeal

This chapter covers:

1. Can you appeal?

2. What decisions can be appealed and who can appeal?

3. Must the decision have been looked at again?

4. What is a mandatory reconsideration?

5. What is the time limit for your appeal?

6. How do you make a valid appeal?

## What you need to know

- You can only appeal against a decision if it carries the right of appeal.

- Most decisions about entitlement can be appealed.

- For most benefits (but not housing benefit), before you can appeal, the decision must usually first have been looked at again and a 'mandatory reconsideration notice' issued by the decision maker. This is expected also to apply to tax credits from April 2014.

- The basic time limit is one month from the date of the decision, but this can be extended in some circumstances.

- Appeals must be made in writing and contain certain information, including grounds for the appeal.

- You should send your appeal to the correct address. Appeals where the decision must first have been looked at again are made directly to HM Courts and Tribunals Service. Housing benefit appeals are made first to the local authority that made the decision.

## 1. Can you appeal?

Before you can appeal against a benefit or tax credit decision:

- you must have been sent a decision notice
- the decision must carry the right of appeal
- usually, the decision maker must have looked at the decision again (carried out a 'mandatory reconsideration') and issued a decision about that (sent to you in a 'mandatory reconsideration notice')

### What is a mandatory reconsideration notice?

For most benefits (but not housing benefit – see page 31) from 28 October 2013, the decision must have been looked at again and a 'mandatory reconsideration notice' issued to you before you can appeal. In such cases, if you wish to appeal, your appeal should be made directly to HM Courts and Tribunals Service. The 'mandatory reconsideration notice' is the letter telling you about the outcome of the decision being looked at again, and tells you whether the decision has been changed or not. It tells you about your right of appeal. The letter may not always have the words 'mandatory reconsideration notice' displayed at the top, but the phrase usually appears in the letter.

For child benefit, guardian's allowance and tax credits cases, it is expected that rules will be introduced from April 2014 requiring that the decision must have been looked at again and a 'mandatory reconsideration notice' issued to you before you can appeal. In such cases, when the appeal is made, you make it directly to HM Courts and Tribunals Service. Before April 2014, however, for child benefit, guardian's allowance and tax credits, there is no requirement for the decision to have been looked at again before you can appeal. Your appeal can be made straight away, and should be sent to the decision maker at HM Revenue and Customs.

There is more information about mandatory reconsiderations later in this chapter.

## 2. Which decisions can be appealed and who can appeal?

Most decisions on benefits and tax credits, including all decisions about your entitlement, carry the right of appeal. You must be given written notice of any decision that can be appealed against.

| Appeal rights | |
| --- | --- |
| Decision | Appeal rights carried |
| Not entitled to employment and support allowance due to failure of the work capability assessment | Yes |
| Entitlement to the employment and support allowance support component | Yes |
| Care needs not sufficient to get personal independence payment | Yes |
| Cannot be paid by cheque | No |
| Not to be paid a budgeting advance | No |
| Does not satisfy the right to reside test | Yes |
| Subject to one-bedroom rate of local housing allowance rather than two-bedroom rate | Yes |
| Subject to a 'bedroom tax' reduction in eligible rent | Yes |
| Benefit sanction for not taking part in a work-focused interview | Yes |
| Income too high for universal credit | Yes |
| Overpayment of benefit or tax credit | Yes |
| Overpayment of universal credit can be recovered | No |

Some decisions cannot be appealed – these are usually about the way your benefit or tax credit is paid, such as when or how payment is made. A few specific decisions, such as about entitlement to a short-term advance of benefit or (for universal credit) a budgeting advance, do not carry the right of appeal.

The notification of your benefit or tax credit entitlement should clearly state whether there is a right of appeal. Disputes about whether you have a right of appeal or not are ultimately decided by HM Courts and Tribunals Service. If you think you have a right of appeal but the decision maker does not, ask that your appeal be forwarded to HM Courts and Tribunals Service. You should state very clearly that you believe there is a right of appeal, and why.

## Can decisions about overpayments be appealed?

*What the law says*

### Appeals about recovering overpayments

Decisions about whether overpayments of **benefits** can be recovered can be appealed except that, since 29 April 2013, decisions about recovery of overpayments of universal credit, and if you can claim universal credit, about contributory employment and support allowance and contribution-based jobseeker's allowance, have not carried the right of appeal. Instead, you must dispute this with the decision maker at the Department for Work and Pensions.

Decisions about whether an overpayment of **tax credits** can be recovered cannot be appealed against. Instead, you must dispute this with the decision maker at HM Revenue and Customs.

*Section 71ZB Social Security Administration Act 1992*

If the tribunal decides that the overpayment can be recovered, the decision to proceed with recovering the overpayment does not have a right of appeal.

### EXAMPLE

**Appealing against an overpayment decision**

Rashid has received a decision saying that he was not entitled to the universal credit he was paid during July and August, and he must repay it.

After the decision is looked at again in a mandatory reconsideration, Rashid can appeal against the decision that he was not entitled to universal credit during July and August. However, he cannot appeal against the decision that he must repay the overpayment. If Rashid accepts that he was not entitled to universal credit, although he cannot appeal about the recovery of the overpayment, he can dispute it with the Department for Work and Pensions (DWP) – for example, on the grounds that recovering the overpayment from him will cause him extreme hardship.

## Who can appeal?

You have the right of appeal as the claimant. Certain other people also have the right of appeal. If any person who can appeal dies, someone can be appointed to proceed with the appeal.

For benefits except housing benefit, people other than you who can appeal are:

- an 'appointee' (someone authorised to act on your behalf)
- someone claiming personal independence payment, disability living allowance or attendance allowance on your behalf if you are terminally ill (even if this is without your knowledge)
- a person from whom an overpayment of benefit, a short-term advance of benefit, a budgeting advance of universal credit or hardship payments can be recovered
- your partner if the decision concerns whether s/he failed to take part in a work-focused interview without good cause
- a person appointed by the DWP or HM Revenue and Customs to proceed with a claim for benefit for someone who has died

For housing benefit, people other than you who can appeal are:

- someone acting for you (for example, an 'appointee') because you cannot act yourself
- someone from whom it has been decided that an overpayment can be recovered, such as a landlord
- a landlord or agent where it has been decided to make, or not to make, payment of housing benefit directly to you

### 3. Must the decision have been looked at again?

From 28 October 2013, for most benefits, the basic rule is that before you have the right of appeal, usually you must apply to the decision maker to look at the decision again and issue another decision about that. If the decision maker has not done this, you do not have the right of appeal.

The process of looking at the decision again is called a 'mandatory reconsideration', and the subsequent decision on the outcome of that process is sent to you in a 'mandatory reconsideration notice'. In the law, the decision on the outcome of the process is actually called a 'revision'.

Box A

**The mandatory reconsideration process**

Step 1: receive a 'decision notice' from the decision maker (it must say that the decision carries the right of appeal after a reconsideration or revision)

Step 2: apply to the decision maker for a mandatory reconsideration

Step 3: receive a mandatory reconsideration notice (revision)

Step 4: send your appeal to HM Courts and Tribunals Service

*What the law says*

**Mandatory reconsiderations**

Where a written decision includes a statement 'to the effect that' a person has the right of appeal only if the decision maker has considered on an application whether to revise the decision, that person only has the right of appeal if the decision maker has 'considered on an application whether to revise the decision'.

*Regulation 7 The Universal Credit, Personal Independence Payment, Jobseeker's Allowance and Employment and Support Allowance (Decisions and Appeals) Regulations 2013; regulation 3ZA Social Security and Child Support (Decisions and Appeals Regulations) 1999*

Box B
**Which benefits does mandatory reconsideration apply to?**

**From 29 April 2013:**

• universal credit
• personal independence payment

**From 28 October 2013:**

• employment and support allowance (contributory and income-related)
• jobseeker's allowance (contribution-based and income-based)
• income support
• pension credit
• attendance allowance
• bereavement benefits
• carer's allowance
• disability living allowance
• industrial injuries benefits
• maternity allowance
• retirement pensions
• social fund budgeting loans, maternity grants, funeral expenses payments, cold weather payments and winter fuel payments

**Expected from April 2014:**

• child benefit
• guardian's allowance
• tax credits (child tax credit and working tax credit)

If mandatory reconsideration applies to you, when you appeal you must send your appeal directly to HM Courts and Tribunals Service, and not to the Department for Work and Pensions (DWP) (or HM Revenue and Customs).

Strictly speaking, a mandatory reconsideration is only required before appeal rights apply where:

• a written notice of the decision has been sent to you

- that written notice says that there is a right of appeal only if an application for a reconsideration (the written notice might actually refer to a 'revision') has been considered, and includes information of the one-month time limit for requesting an 'any grounds' revision and (if the decision does not already include a statement of reasons) that a statement of reasons can be requested if requested within one month

From 28 October 2013, most decision notices will contain this information, as well as whether the decision carries the right of appeal. Where the decision does not include all of this information, you could argue that you can appeal directly against the decision without having to have had it looked at again.

**Box C**
**Benefit appeals before 28 October 2013**

- Before 28 October 2013, for most benefits you could appeal against a decision without having to have the decision looked at again.

- Under these rules, your appeal was sent first to the decision maker (for example, at the DWP) rather than directly to HM Courts and Tribunals Service.

- The official appeal form was Form GL24 for appeals sent to the DWP or Form CH24A for child benefit and guardian's allowance appeals to HM Revenue and Customs.

- On receipt of your appeal, the decision maker considered whether s/he should change the decision appealed against; if not, a response was prepared and the appeal was then sent to HM Courts and Tribunals Service.

- Other rules, for example about time limits and the way the appeal is dealt with, were the same as they are now.

If you appealed under these arrangements, you do not have to go back and have the decision looked at again now, and your appeal will continue.

## Do housing benefit decisions need to be looked at again?

For housing benefit, there is no need for a mandatory reconsideration before an appeal can be made. If the decision carries the right of appeal, an appeal can be made straight away.

Appeals should be sent to the decision maker at the local authority within one month, although late appeals are possible. Official appeal forms are available from your local authority (but you do not have to use the official form). The local authority prepares a response to the appeal before passing the papers to HM Courts and Tribunals Service.

There is still the option of asking for the decision to be looked at again first, but this is not mandatory. If you ask for this within one month, you do not need to satisfy grounds for getting the decision looked at again.

Asking for the decision to be looked at again is one way of avoiding an appeal. However, unless the local authority has made a very simple and obvious mistake in its decision, it may be better to appeal straight away. If there is an appeal, the local authority should look again at the decision anyway. But if the local authority does not actually change the decision, the appeal will need to continue if you still want to get the decision changed.

## What are the rules for child benefit, guardian's allowance and tax credits?

For child benefit, guardian's allowance and tax credits, it is expected that from April 2014 you will have to have a mandatory reconsideration by a decision maker at HM Revenue and Customs before you can appeal against a decision. Before then, however, if the decision carries the right of appeal, then you can appeal to the First-tier Tribunal straight away.

From April 2014, the rules on mandatory reconsideration for child benefit and guardian's allowance are expected to be the same as those that apply to other benefits. It is expected that there will be new rules on mandatory reconsiderations for tax credits.

## 4. What is a mandatory reconsideration?

A mandatory reconsideration is the process by which the decision maker looks again at the decision you are unhappy about, after you have applied for this. If the decision maker accepts your application and looks again at the decision, s/he sends you a decision on the outcome of that in a mandatory reconsideration notice.

As part of the mandatory reconsideration process, the decision maker may contact you by telephone and ask if you have any further evidence to send in before s/he makes a decision.

Official letters and leaflets may refer to the whole process of looking at a decision again and the resulting decision as a 'reconsideration'. However, the law describes the actual decision you get following a *mandatory* reconsideration, and which is sent to you in the mandatory reconsideration notice, as a '**revision**'. So in effect, where the mandatory reconsideration rules apply you must have a revision before you can appeal.

### What is the time limit for requesting a mandatory reconsideration?

Your request for the decision to be looked at again must be received by the decision maker within one month of the date the decision notice was sent to you. If your request is made within this time limit, a mandatory reconsideration is then carried out and a decision (a revision) is sent to you in a mandatory reconsideration notice. (If your request is within the basic time limit, the revision does not require particular grounds to be carried out, and so is called an 'any grounds' revision.)

*What the law says*

#### What is a 'month' for the purpose of these rules?

This is a calendar month. For example, one calendar month from 1 June is 1 July.

*Schedule 1 Interpretation Act 1978; paragraph 03063 DWP Decision Maker's Guide*

The one-month time limit can be extended if a statement of reasons is not already included with the decision, and is requested within one month of the date the decision was sent. But for most decisions, officials regard the decision as already containing a statement of reasons, and will not adjust the time limit for asking for a revision if a statement is requested. For example, the Department for Work and Pensions (DWP) regards decisions about whether the work capability assessment is satisfied, or whether the disability tests for personal independence payment are satisfied, as already containing a statement of reasons.

### EXAMPLE

#### Applying for a mandatory reconsideration

Javed received a decision saying that he was not entitled to employment and support allowance as he did not satisfy the work capability assessment. The decision was sent to Javed on 1 November 2013. The decision contains a statement of reasons.

Javed thinks he should pass the work capability assessment, as he thinks he scores sufficient points, and also thinks that being required to look for work would be a danger to his health. On 25 November 2013, he requests that the decision maker at the DWP looks at the decision again. As that is received within the basic time limit of one month for an 'any grounds' revision, he does not need to prove anything more for a mandatory reconsideration to be carried out.

A decision maker at the DWP carries out a mandatory reconsideration. The decision is not changed as the decision maker considers that the original decision was correct. That is notified in writing to Javed in a mandatory reconsideration notice. Javed can now appeal against the decision to the First-tier Tribunal.

If a statement of reasons is requested within a month of the date the decision was sent, and it is agreed that one needs to be sent, the one-month time limit is extended. If the written statement of reasons is actually provided within a month of the decision, the time limit for requesting a revision is extended to one month and 14 days. If the written statement is not provided within a month of the decision, the time limit is within 14 days of the written statement being provided.

**Have you missed the time limit?**

You may be able to get a mandatory reconsideration even if you do not ask for the decision to be looked at again within the basic time limit. This is because sometimes a 'late revision' of the decision is possible. If your application for a late revision is refused, no mandatory reconsideration notice is issued and you have no right of appeal.

If you are asking for your decision to be looked at again after the basic one-month time limit, make it clear that you are making a late request for a revision. A late revision can be carried out on 'any grounds' if you ask for it within an absolute time limit of:

- if the decision is about personal independence payment, or you are on or able to apply for universal credit, 13 months of the date . the basic one-month time limit expired
- otherwise, 13 months from the date of notification of the decision

An application for a late revision should enable the decision to be identified, and include a summary of your reasons why your application is late.

For decisions made on or after 28 October 2013, for a late revision to be carried out on any grounds, the decision maker also needs to be satisfied that:

- it is reasonable to grant the late revision, *and*
- there are 'special circumstances' (these are not defined) why the revision could not be made in time

If it is too late for you to have a late revision on any grounds, there are limited grounds for a late revision without any time limit at all. These are referred to as 'any time' revisions. However, the grounds are very limited, and it is often difficult to persuade the decision maker to carry out an 'any time' revision. If the decision maker refuses to carry out an 'any time' revision, you do not get a mandatory reconsideration notice and you do not have the right of appeal. Again, it is best to make it clear that you are asking for a late revision, and say how you satisfy the grounds for such a revision.

---

**EXAMPLE**

**Applying for a late revision**

On 5 December 2013, Marion was sent a decision about her personal independence payment, saying she was not entitled to the mobility component as she could walk and did not need anyone with her when she was out.

Marion suffers from extreme anxiety and depression, and the decision came at a bad time. She was too unwell to do anything about it until 10 May 2014, when she went to her local advice centre for help. The advice centre helped her to make a late request for a revision, explaining that it was late because Marion was in a period of particular bad health during the month after receiving the decision and had not been able to deal with any correspondence. A letter from her GP is enclosed confirming this. Also, her health problems have always meant that she needs a companion when she goes out, something that had always been accepted in the past and had not got any better.

The decision maker at the DWP accepts the late request for a revision. The decision maker upholds the original decision so that Marion still does not get the mobility component. But, as a revision has been carried out, Marion is sent that decision in a mandatory reconsideration notice. She can now appeal to the First-tier Tribunal.

---

An 'any time' revision can be carried out on the grounds of:

- 'official error' – see Box D
- mistake or ignorance about a fact that is relevant to the claim, *but* only if the decision was more favourable to you because of that. So this ground will not help you if you think that the decision on

your claim is wrong but you are too late to request an any grounds revision. In practice, this ground for an 'any time' revision is used by the decision maker where s/he wants to reduce your entitlement

**Box D**
**What is an 'official error'?**

An official error is made by the DWP, HM Revenue and Customs or local authority and can be a:

- mistake about the law (but not if that is only because it has been shown to be wrong by a later Upper Tribunal or court decision)
- failure to take into account specific, relevant evidence
- failure to pass written evidence received by the department to the decision maker
- failure to ask about something that was relevant (but not if it is about not keeping your claim under constant review, or not raising things not raised by you)

### What if you cannot get a revision?

If you have a current award of the benefit (not tax credit), it may be possible to have the decision changed by a 'supersession' for a mistake or ignorance about a relevant fact, or on the basis of a relevant change in your circumstances. Even if a supersession is made in your favour, you will not get full backdating. If the mandatory reconsideration rules apply, you cannot appeal against a decision on a supersession. You must still have a revision before you can appeal.

### Do you have a mandatory reconsideration notice?

A mandatory reconsideration notice is the letter notifying you that a decision has been looked at again. Where the decision has the right of appeal, the mandatory reconsideration notice should say so. If it does not, but you consider that there should be a right of appeal, it is up to HM Courts and Tribunals Service to decide.

Once the mandatory reconsideration notice has been received, if you still wish to appeal then an appeal can be made to HM Courts and Tribunals Service.

The date the mandatory reconsideration notice is sent is the date from which the time limit for your appeal starts. A copy of the notice should be included with your appeal (although the tribunal can ignore ('waive') that requirement if it considers that is right to do so).

**Box E**
**Mandatory reconsiderations and time limits**

- If you think you may want to appeal, ask for your decision to be looked at again within the basic one-month time limit (so that you get a revision on 'any grounds'). That way, you are guaranteed to get a mandatory reconsideration notice and have the right of appeal. You do not have to give grounds for your request, but making a strong case for why the decision should be changed is still helpful, as it may prevent the need to appeal.

- If it has not been possible to make your request with the basic time limit, consider asking for a late revision (within 13 months). You are not guaranteed a right of appeal, as the decision maker may refuse to carry out a revision. Ample explanation of the lateness and sending in supportive evidence would help.

- If all else is lost, consider whether a late revision at 'any time' is possible. In practice, this is restricted to cases of clear 'official error' (see Box D). You are not guaranteed a right of appeal, as the decision maker may refuse to carry out a revision.

## 5. What is the time limit for your appeal?

Your appeal must be:

- made on time, which means it is within the time limit

- valid, which means it must be in writing and include the necessary information

## What is the time limit for a benefits appeal?

For benefit decisions, the basic time limit is one calendar month. Time runs from the date the decision in the mandatory reconsideration notice, or (where mandatory reconsideration does not apply) from the date the original decision was sent to you. Note that the appeal must be *received* within this time limit – it is not enough for you just to have sent it within that time.

*What the law says*

**Benefit appeal time limits**

The basic time limit is one month.

One month = one calendar month.

The absolute time limit for a late appeal is 13 months.

*Rule 22 The Tribunal Procedure (First-tier Tribunal) (Social Entitlement Chamber) Rules 2008; R(IB) 4/02 (a decision of the Social Security Commissioner)*

**EXAMPLE**

### Appealing after getting a mandatory reconsideration notice

A mandatory reconsideration notice is sent to Charlie on 4 November. The original decision is not changed by the decision maker. Charlie wants to appeal.

The standard time limit for Charlie to make his appeal expires at the end of 4 December – one month after the date of the decision in the mandatory reconsideration notice. His appeal must be received at HM Courts and Tribunals Service within that time.

## What is the time limit for a housing benefit appeal?

For housing benefit, and any other benefit decision where a mandatory reconsideration is not required, the basic time limit is that your appeal must be received within one month from the date of issue of the original decision. A late appeal may be possible.

The basic time limit can be extended if a written statement of reasons is requested within the month and it is agreed that the decision did not already contain such reasons. Note, however, that in most cases the original decision is regarded as already containing reasons.

Where a written statement is supplied, the basic time limit is extended by 14 days from the end of the month or (if this is a later date) 14 days from the date on which the written statement of reasons was sent. If a revision (one that was not mandatory) has been carried out, the basic time limit is one month from the date of issue of the decision on that.

## What is the time limit for a tax credit appeal?

*What the law says*

### Tax credit time limits

An appeal must be given within 30 days of the decision.

*Section 39(1) Tax Credits Act 2002*

For tax credits, the basic time limit is 30 days from the date on which the decision was given. Your appeal must be received within this time limit. Currently, caselaw has decided that the tribunal has no power to extend this time limit so that your appeal can be considered even if it is late, although rules are meant to allow you an additional 12 months to make a late appeal. However, if your tax credits appeal is late, insist that you must be allowed to have a late appeal considered in order for your right to a fair trial to be complied with. It is understood that HM Revenue and Customs is continuing to allow late appeals to be admitted, and may amend the rules in the future to clarify that they are possible.

**What the law says**

### Extending tax credit time limits

The tribunal has no power to extend the time limit for a tax credit appeal so as to allow a late appeal.

*JI v Commissioners for HM Revenue and Customs (TC) [2013] UKUT 199 (AAC) (a decision of the Upper Tribunal)*

## What if your appeal is late?

If you miss the basic time limit, you may be able to make a late appeal.

| Time limit for making a late appeal | |
| --- | --- |
| Type of decision | Time limit |
| Benefits | 13 months from the date of notification of the decision (for example, the decision in the mandatory reconsideration notice) |
| Tax credits | 12 months from the date the 30-day basic time limit ended, although caselaw has decided that currently this cannot apply |

The tribunal makes the decision on whether your appeal should be allowed to go ahead but it must apply the time limit for making a late appeal. It is not bound by any special rules. The main principle it has to apply is to ensure that your appeal request is considered 'fairly and justly'.

**What the law says**

### Late appeals

The First-tier Tribunal makes the ultimate decision on whether an appeal can go ahead and is not restricted in what it can take into account. The appeal will go ahead if the decision maker (or anyone else with the right of appeal) does not object and the tribunal does not decide otherwise.

*Rules 22(8) and 23(4) The Tribunal Procedure (First-tier Tribunal) (Social Entitlement Chamber) Rules 2008*

If the decision maker does not object, your appeal is allowed to go ahead, unless the tribunal decides otherwise (it is unusual for the tribunal to do this). But even if the decision maker objects, the tribunal can still decide that your appeal should go ahead. If the decision maker objects to your late appeal being allowed to go ahead, the tribunal may write to you and give you a chance to comment, before making its decision.

---

**EXAMPLE**

**Requesting a late appeal**

Morag received a decision dated 21 May saying that she was not entitled to personal independence payment. Morag disagreed with the decision and asked for it to be looked at again (a mandatory reconsideration). Morag's request for the decision to be looked at again was received on 15 June. Although a mandatory reconsideration was carried out, the decision was not changed. The decision (in a mandatory reconsideration notice) was sent to Morag on 9 July.

After getting the mandatory reconsideration notice, Morag had an accident at home which resulted in her having to spend time in hospital. Because of that, she did not appeal until 2 September. This was outside the basic one-month period starting on 9 July, but within the absolute 13-month period.

Morag stated in her appeal form that she was appealing late because the accident and hospital stay had made it difficult to appeal within the month. She also said that she felt her appeal had strong merits because her GP could confirm that she needed a lot of help at home even before her accident.

The decision maker at the DWP did not object to the appeal going ahead. The First-tier Tribunal decided that the late appeal should be accepted. It went on to consider Morag's appeal and whether she qualified for personal independence payment.

If the tribunal refuses to accept your late appeal, the appeal cannot go ahead. You can appeal against the refusal to accept the late appeal to the Upper Tribunal (but note that the Upper Tribunal cannot decide that the time limit for making a late appeal did not apply).

In practice, it is often possible to have a late appeal accepted. However, there is no guarantee that this will happen.

No appeal can be accepted if it is more than 13 months after the decision being appealed against was sent. Where there has been a mandatory reconsideration, that means 13 months from the date the decision in the mandatory reconsideration notice was sent to you.

If you request a late appeal, state that clearly on the letter or appeal form. Also include the reasons why your appeal is late, and why it is important that the appeal should be allowed to go ahead. This is not defined in the rules, and could include things like illness or language problems. Also, things like the strength of your case, the amount of money at stake or not being able to get advice may be relevant.

## 6. How do you make a valid appeal?

*What the law says*

**The basic rules**

To be valid, your appeal must:
* be in writing (in English or in Welsh)
* signed by you
* include certain information

*Rules 22 and 23 The Tribunal Procedure (First-tier Tribunal) (Social Entitlement Chamber) Rules 2008; regulation 20 The Housing Benefit and Council Tax Benefit (Decisions and Appeals) Regulations 2001*

If you have a representative and there is written notification of this, including your representative's name and address, s/he can sign the appeal form for you. To avoid complication, however, it is always preferable if you, as the claimant, sign the appeal.

Although your appeal must be in writing, it does not have to be on the official appeal form. However, using the appeal form is preferable as it sets out the necessary details and information in a helpful way.

**What information must be included?**

Box F
**Information that must be provided**

- Your details, and those of your representative if you have one.

- The grounds of the appeal. This is a summary of the reasons why the decision is wrong. The official form usually has a large box to put these details in.

- The address where the appeal documents can be sent to – this can be your representative's address, but check with your representative first.

- Except in housing benefit cases, a copy of the decision appealed against (usually, the mandatory reconsideration notice).

- Except in housing benefit cases, any documents in support of the appeal which the decision maker does not already have.

For housing benefit cases, although you do not need to provide a copy of the decision being appealed against, you do still need to identify it – for example, by including the date of the original decision.

The official appeal form from HM Courts and Tribunals Service also asks for some other additional information, such as your national insurance number and whether you would like to have an oral hearing. Where you request an oral hearing, there are further questions about the arrangements for that – for example, about dates on which you are unavailable or if you have any particular needs at the tribunal venue, such as a hearing loop or an interpreter.

The official appeal form from the local authority in housing benefit cases may ask for similar additional information.

Further details can always be provided at a later date.

### What if all the information cannot be included?

The First-tier Tribunal has the power to ignore (or 'waive') things that are normally required if it considers that 'fair or just'. For example, if you do not have an actual copy of your mandatory reconsideration notice, supplying details such as the date of the decision, your national insurance number and the benefit concerned may be enough, although it is up to the tribunal to decide.

Basic requirements such as the need to supply relevant names and addresses are likely to be more difficult things for the tribunal to ignore.

### Do you have to use the official appeal form?

Although it is not essential to use an official appeal form to make your appeal, using one, where possible, is recommended. A local authority may insist that you use its official appeal form – though ultimately the decision on whether your appeal is valid is always made by the First-tier Tribunal, not the local authority.

Some advice agencies keep copies of the form, so your representative may have a copy to hand.

If you use a form other than an SSCS1 to make your appeal where you do need to have had a mandatory reconsideration, it is understood that HM Courts and Tribunals Service will accept it, as long as you include your mandatory reconsideration notice.

## Appeal forms

| Type of decision | Form | Available from |
|---|---|---|
| Most benefits, where there is a need to have had a mandatory reconsideration before appealing (universal credit, personal independence payment, and most other benefits from 28 October 2013) | SSCS1 | www.justice.gov.uk and www.gov.uk |
| For DWP benefits without a need for a mandatory reconsideration before appealing (decisions made before 28 October 2013) | GL24, 'If You Think Our Decision is Wrong' | www.justice.gov.uk and www.gov.uk |
| Housing benefit | local authority's own appeal form | local authority |
| Child benefit and guardian's allowance decisions made by HM Revenue and Customs | CH24A, 'If You Think Our Decision is Wrong' | www.hmrc.gov.uk |
| Tax credits | WTC/AP, 'What to Do if You Think Your Child Tax Credit/Working Tax Credit is Wrong' | www.hmrc.gov.uk |

## What are the 'grounds' for your appeal?

The grounds for an appeal are simply the reasons that your appeal is being made – why you disagree with the decision being appealed against.

The grounds for your appeal do not need to be technical. But they do need to state why the appeal is being made and show why you think the decision is wrong.

- Grounds for your appeal do not need to be lengthy, but should be as clear as possible. Just indicating disagreement probably is not enough.

- Try to identify the particular reasons why the decision is wrong.

- There is no requirement to specify particular parts of the law (for example, exactly what descriptor(s) in the work capability assessment is or are being argued for), but if you can be specific about that there is no harm in doing so.

- Any evidence in support of the appeal that you have but the decision maker does not must be sent in with the appeal. It is advisable to send in any evidence as soon as it is available and keep a copy and a record of posting. If there is something obviously wrong with the evidence used to make the decision, such as an inadequate medical examination, say so.

## EXAMPLES

### Grounds for the appeal

I am appealing against this decision as I think I am too ill to work, and so should be entitled to employment and support allowance, because of my walking problems and arthritis.

- I can't walk more than about 20 metres without having to stop because I am so out of breath, and after that I can only walk about the same again before having to stop altogether. I don't use a wheelchair as I have not been recommended one by my doctor.

- Because of my arthritis I can't stand or sit for long before having to move about.

I disagree with the decision that I am not entitled to personal independence payment. I think I am entitled to the daily living part because of the amount of help I need during the day.

I put on the form that I need a lot of help during the day with things like washing and dressing, and with cooking and eating, and with dealing with bills and letters, several times a day. I need a lot of prompting and encouragement to do these things because of my depression and anxiety. But the doctor that was sent to see me did not ask much about that, and the decision seems to have ignored what I said.

## If your appeal is not valid

In most benefit cases except housing benefit, where there has been a mandatory reconsideration and your appeal is made directly to the tribunal, only the First-tier Tribunal can consider whether your appeal is valid. If the tribunal thinks there is not enough information in your appeal to make it valid, it can ask you to provide more information. If you used the official appeal form, it is sent back to you for more information to be added. It is very important to comply as far as possible with what the tribunal asks for. Otherwise, the tribunal may decide that your appeal is not valid, and (if it has indicated that this is possible), it may cancel ('strike out') the appeal. If an appeal is struck out, it does not go ahead. A decision to strike your appeal out can be appealed to the Upper Tribunal.

For housing benefit appeals, the local authority decision maker can return the appeal form for completion or request that further information is supplied for the appeal to be valid.

In other benefit cases where there is no requirement for a mandatory reconsideration, the decision maker can request the appeal form be completed or that further information be supplied for the appeal to be valid. The vast majority of such cases are decisions about benefits other than universal credit or personal independence payment dated before 28 October 2013.

Where there is not a requirement for mandatory reconsideration and the decision maker returns the appeal form or requests further information, the basic time limit for appealing is extended by 14 days or longer if allowed.

If the decision maker's request is not complied with, s/he must forward the matter to the First-tier Tribunal – only the tribunal can make the ultimate decision on whether your appeal is valid.

## Where should you send your appeal?

Where you must have a mandatory reconsideration before you can appeal, when you do appeal, send your appeal to HM Courts and Tribunals Service. This is sometimes called 'direct lodgement'.

## Where to send your appeal

| Type of decision | Send to |
| --- | --- |
| Where you must have had a mandatory reconsideration notice before you can appeal (most benefits) | HM Courts and Tribunals Service<br>In England and Wales: HMCTS SSCS Appeals Centre, PO Box 1203, Bradford BD1 9WP<br>In Scotland: HMCTS SSCS Appeals Centre, PO Box 27080, Glasgow G2 9HQ |
| Benefits where there is no need for a mandatory reconsideration notice before you can appeal (decisions before 28 October 2013, child benefit and guardian's allowance probably until April 2014) | The decision maker |
| Housing benefit | The local authority that made the decision |
| Tax credits where there is no need for have a mandatory reconsideration notice before you can appeal | HM Revenue and Customs |
| Tax credits where you must have had a mandatory reconsideration notice before you can appeal (expected to be from April 2014) | HM Courts and Tribunals Service |

## Further information

For more details about revisions and supersessions, see CPAG's *Welfare Benefits and Tax Credits Handbook*.

Official guidance and appeal forms can be found at CPAG's appeals toolkit (www.cpag.org.uk/appeals-toolkit).

# Chapter 4
# Preparing your appeal

**This chapter covers:**

1. What are tribunals like?

2. Do you have a representative?

3. How do you prepare your appeal?

4. What is the point of the appeal?

5. How do you check the law?

6. How do you gather facts and evidence?

7. How do you write a submission?

## What you need to know

- First-tier Tribunals are 'inquisitorial', meaning they are particularly concerned with establishing facts and considering evidence in order to get at the truth.

- It is strongly advisable to get a representative to help you with your appeal if you can.

- Submitting further evidence where possible, especially medical evidence, may be important to winning your appeal.

- At an oral hearing, the tribunal will get evidence from you by questioning you directly, and that is often key to winning your appeal.

- The basic steps for preparing your appeal are identifying the point of your appeal, checking relevant law, gathering facts and evidence and writing a brief submission.

## 1. What are tribunals like?

### The nature of the tribunal

The tribunal has an 'inquisitorial' role. This means that it is concerned with establishing facts and considering evidence to establish the truth, and then applying the relevant law to make its decision. The tribunal asks questions (at an oral hearing) and considers the strengths and weaknesses of the evidence. In doing this, the tribunal is more like an inquiry rather than a contest. For more about the tribunal hearing, see Chapter 6.

Although the tribunal is a court of law, it is different from most other courts. Other courts, such as a criminal court, have an 'adversarial' nature where cross-examination may take place and one side may have to prove their case 'beyond reasonable doubt'.

In contrast to an adversarial court, the tribunal ideally is a discussion between the parties to the appeal rather than a conflict between two opposing sides, and so is supposed to be relatively informal. The tribunal itself does most of the questioning, and there is no cross-examination. In the rare cases where one side has to prove its case, there is no requirement to prove the case 'beyond reasonable doubt'. Rather, the test (called the 'burden of proof') is simply whether on 'the balance of probability' it is more likely to be true than not.

The tribunal is supposed to be relatively informal. Certainly, it should not be as formal or potentially intimidating as a criminal or other adversarial court. The tribunal members do not wear judicial wigs or gowns, and questioning, although very much part of the process, is supposed to get at the truth rather than just prove a particular point. Oaths are not usually required, although the tribunal can use them if it wishes to. All the parties to the appeal, including you, are supposed to assist the tribunal in establishing the facts rather than just trying to discredit the case made by the 'other side'. The tribunal must deal with cases 'fairly and justly'.

What the law says

### The nature of tribunals

The overriding objective of the tribunal rules is to deal with cases 'fairly and justly'. That includes 'avoiding unnecessary formality and seeking flexibility in the proceedings' and 'ensuring, so far as practicable, that the parties are able to participate fully in the proceedings'.

*Rule 2 The Tribunal Procedure (First-tier Tribunal) (Social Entitlement Chamber) Rules 2008*

Remember that the tribunal is still a court of law. In an oral hearing, the tribunal will ask you questions about the facts of your case. The questioning may be about personal matters and can often be quite direct and to the point. Some tribunals can therefore seem very business-like and even somewhat brusque. Usually, the tribunal asks far fewer questions of your representative, if you have one. It may ask your representative to outline why the appeal has been made and if s/he wants to make any further points, but will not want her/him to give your evidence if you are capable of doing so.

## 2. Do you have a representative?

What the law says

### Representatives

A party to the appeal may appoint a representative (whether a legal representative or not) to represent her/him.

Once notified, a representative is assumed to be authorised to represent, and s/he must be sent any document which the person s/he is representing is be sent.

Parties to the appeal must help the tribunal to 'further the overriding objective' of dealing with cases fairly and justly, and generally 'co-operate with the tribunal'.

*Rules 2 and 11 The Tribunal Procedure (First-tier Tribunal) (Social Entitlement Chamber) Rules 2008*

You and the decision maker (for example, at the Department for Work and Pensions) are 'parties' to the appeal. As a 'party' to the appeal, you have a right to be represented by any person, whether s/he is a lawyer or not. You do not have to have a representative, but it is strongly advisable to get one if you can, as s/he can help prepare your appeal.

Your representative's name and address should be notified to the tribunal. The tribunal can, if it wishes, still allow someone who has not been notified to represent. A representative has the same rights and responsibilities (for instance, to a fair hearing) as any party to the appeal. In particular, that means s/he must help the tribunal in dealing with the case and co-operate with the tribunal.

Once you have notified that you have a representative, s/he is presumed to be acting for you unless you notify in writing that this is no longer the case. Your representative should be sent any documents about your appeal.

**What is the role of the representative?**

There are few actual rules about representatives and their role before the tribunal. However, there is general consent about what tribunals usually expect from a representative (see Box A).

Box A
**What is your representative expected to do?**

- S/he is not expected to be a legal expert. However, s/he is expected to know the case s/he wants to make, ideally set out in a written submission. It is an advantage for her/him to know about the relevant law at issue in the appeal. Your representative is not there just as a companion to you.

- S/he should be able to say how the relevant facts and evidence support your case. For example, why the official medical report is inadequate or how the letter obtained from your GP is supportive. Tribunals often like this set out in a written submission.

- S/he is expected to have prepared you for the appeal hearing so that you know that you will be questioned about the facts of your case –for instance, about your illness and how it affects you.

- S/he should be polite and co-operative. Your representative is expected to assist the tribunal rather than attack the 'other side', and aggressive conduct is disapproved of. However, that does not mean that s/he should not be assertive when pointing out the strengths of your case, or about pointing out flaws in the decision that is being appealed against.

At an oral hearing, the tribunal is unlikely to ask many questions of your representative, as it wants to spend most time talking directly to you. The tribunal will ask your representative to summarise what decision you are seeking and why. So, in an appeal about the work capability assessment, it normally expects your representative to say what points you are asking the tribunal to award, or otherwise on what basis the work capability assessment is satisfied. Your representative should be able to do that in a brief and concise way. Tribunals usually prefer this in a few sentences and bullet points in a written submission, ideally sent in advance of the hearing.

In general, the tribunal is able to rely on your representative to state the case and the decision you are asking for. This may mean that the tribunal does not consider things that your representative has not argued for.

**EXAMPLE**

**What decision is being sought?**

Ben's appeal is about personal independence payment. His representative says that there is no dispute about the decision regarding the daily living component, but wants to argue for the mobility component. The tribunal leaves the daily living component out of consideration (although it does not actually *have* to).

If your representative has not had time to prepare properly, for example because s/he has been asked to represent at very short notice, s/he should make sure that the tribunal knows that.

Generally speaking, the tribunal is supposed to apply the relevant law itself. So if your representative attempts to instruct the tribunal about the relevant law, it may not be looked upon favourably. However, most tribunals have no objection to a mention of law or caselaw where it is particularly relevant to the case. For example, your representative may want to mention some caselaw about the application of a particular descriptor in the work capability assessment because it involves very similar facts to those in your own case, and has not been mentioned in the appeal papers.

However, knowing about the law relevant to the appeal is important, even if it is not the subject of any specific part of your representative's submission to the tribunal, as it helps her/him to understand what facts are relevant and what evidence you may need.

## 3. How do you prepare your appeal?

There is nothing in the law that says what you must or must not do to prepare your appeal. But in any appeal the basic steps are very likely to be the same. If you follow these basic steps, you can go to the appeal hearing knowing that you have prepared for it well. Good preparation is one of the keys to winning your appeal.

Box B
**Preparing the appeal – five basic steps**

1. Identify the **point of the appeal**. What is your appeal about and what decision are you asking the tribunal to make?

2. Check the **law and caselaw** relevant to the point of your appeal.

3. Establish the **facts** relevant to the point of your appeal, and where possible gather further **evidence** relevant to the point of your appeal.

4. Write a brief **submission** setting out what you are asking the tribunal to do and how the facts and evidence support your case.

5. Ensure that there is an **oral hearing**. The tribunal can ask you questions at the hearing about the facts of your case. Ideally, your representative will be at the hearing too.

## If you can get a representative

Your representative can help prepare your appeal. Preparing for an appeal ideally involves the methods described in Boxes A and B, which includes things like gathering evidence, checking the law and writing a submission. A good representative can provide a lot of help with this and the other steps in preparing an appeal.

## If you cannot get a representative

If you cannot get a representative, you can still try to prepare your appeal in the using the stages in Box B. If doing all that is difficult for you, try to do the following:

- get further evidence to support your appeal if you can – for example, a letter from your GP
- ask for an oral hearing of your appeal and attend the hearing
- prepare to be questioned about the facts of your case

# 4. What is the point of the appeal?

The 'point of the appeal' is the very basic matter of what your appeal is about – the decision that you are unhappy about, and what decision you are asking the tribunal to put in its place. In most cases, the point of your appeal is just about one or two things.

Knowing the point of your appeal as early as possible is vital so you (or your representative) can start to think about which facts and other information are relevant, and what evidence to get. Also, once you are clear about what the point of the appeal is, you are much better able to narrow down your search for what the relevant law and caselaw is.

A point of the appeal is also useful when thinking about the mass of information that is usually involved in an appeal to the tribunal. The appeal papers sent out to you before the hearing nearly always have a lot of things about the history of your claim, claim forms, copies of decisions, as well as a 'submission' from the decision maker in your case, which is a statement of how the decision under appeal was made and what the tribunal may want to do. This can amount to a bewildering amount of information. Try not to worry when you first see a set of appeal papers.

## EXAMPLES

### The point of the appeal

John has been refused employment and support allowance because he fails the work capability assessment. He believes more points should be awarded in the mental health part of the assessment, and these are sufficient so that the assessment is satisfied. The work capability assessment points John is asking for in particular are in the activity for coping with change.

Angela has been refused housing benefit because the tenancy is 'contrived' or is not on a 'commercial basis'. But the tenancy was created to provide her with a home, and there is an agreement to pay a reasonable rent to the landlord. So Angela is arguing that the tenancy is not contrived, and is on a commercial basis.

Anne has been told that she is not entitled to tax credits as a single person because she is living together with another person as husband and wife. Anne says that her alleged cohabitee has not lived in the property for two years, and in any case they were only ever friends, so they have never lived together as husband and wife.

Henri has been refused universal credit because he does not have the right to reside. However, he was working part time before falling ill and should have a right to reside on the basis that he has retained his status as worker.

Once you have identified the point of the appeal, you will see that a lot of the information in the appeal papers is really background material, and in fact only certain parts of it are relevant to the point of the appeal.

Think of all the information in the appeal as like a pyramid, with a lot of background information at the base of the pyramid, some partly relevant material in the middle, but most of the directly relevant material occupying just the top part of the pyramid. This top part of the pyramid is the part that relates to the point of the appeal. If you concentrate on the material relevant to the point of the appeal, the mass of information will not seem intimidating.

## How do you identify the point of your appeal?

Usually, you can identify the point of your appeal by looking carefully at why the decision you want to appeal against makes you unhappy. If you have a representative, s/he should talk to you about things that may have gone wrong – for example, if you feel that you had a poor quality medical assessment, or that you didn't put down enough information in your claim form or questionnaire. In practice, it is very difficult to be clear about the point of the appeal without doing these things.

The decision itself may identify very clearly what the point of your appeal will be. For example, if you have been refused employment and support allowance, the decision may state that it has been refused because you failed the work capability assessment and include a list of the points that have been awarded (and not awarded) in the assessment.

Much more information about the appeal is available in the appeal papers that are sent out to you by the decision maker. They include not only the decision under appeal, but also copies of your claim forms, medical reports and the submission, including references to the law from the decision maker. However, relatively speaking, the appeal papers may not be issued until shortly before the appeal is heard. It is unwise to leave it to this point before preparing.

## 5. How do you check the law?

The First-tier Tribunal knows about the law relevant to your appeal. Most appeals do not involve complex legal issues. The tribunal does not expect you to know about the law, and does not expect your representative, if you have one, to be a legal expert. However, the tribunal does expect your representative to know about the basic law that is relevant to your appeal.

In making its decision, the tribunal must apply the relevant law; it has no discretion to ignore or alter it. It will help you to know about the relevant law to understand what the tribunal can and cannot do in your case.

*What CPAG says*

### Looking up the law

Social security law can sometimes be complex, and looking up the law relevant to the appeal is an important part of preparation. However, many claimants have very limited resources and have circumstances in which checking the law is difficult. A good representative is able to check the law for you and will have the tools necessary to do so.

If you cannot get a representative, checking the basic law yourself, using the advice in this chapter, could also help you to think about the sort of facts and evidence that are relevant to you case.

### What is social security law?

Social security law consists of two main things:

- legislation such as Acts of Parliament and regulations
- caselaw such as decisions of the Upper Tribunal (formerly known as the Social Security and Child Support Commissioners), Court of Appeal, Supreme Court (formerly House of Lords) and the European courts

**Legislation** sets out the rules. Acts of Parliament set out the main rules in numbered sections. Regulations set out more detailed rules. Again they are numbered and may have subparagraphs.

**Caselaw** clarifies how the rules in the legislation are to be applied, for instance what the meaning of particular words or concepts in the regulations should be.

The most common caselaw is in the form of decisions of the Upper Tribunal. The First-tier Tribunal must follow the decisions of the Upper Tribunal. Upper Tribunal decisions have reference numbers called 'neutral citation numbers' in which the name of the claimant is abbreviated, sometimes along with that of the Secretary of State for Work and Pensions (SSWP). The Upper Tribunal (UKUT) and the name of the benefit are also abbreviated.

---

**EXAMPLE**

**Identifying an Upper Tribunal decision**

*ML v SSWP (ESA)* [2012] UKUT 503 (AAC) is the neutral citation number of an Upper Tribunal decision about employment and support allowance from 2012, in which the claimant's initials were ML and the decision maker whose decision was under appeal was the Secretary of State for Work and Pensions.

---

If the decision is considered to be of particular importance, it is 'reported'. In such cases, the neutral citation number then includes an additional reference at the end which can be identified by the letter 'R' (for reported). If an unreported decision conflicts with a reported decision, the reported decision is normally applied.

A decision made by a three-judge panel of the Upper Tribunal is given preference to a decision made by a single Upper Tribunal judge.

In a few cases, caselaw is from the higher courts – the Court of Appeal, the Supreme Court (formerly the House of Lords), the Scottish Court of Session or the European Court of Justice. They take precedence over decisions of the Upper Tribunal.

Before the Upper Tribunal was created, the judges that made the decisions there were known as Social Security and Child Support Commissioners – usually shortened to Social Security Commissioners. The decisions they made had different references. For example, CIB/14587/1996 was a decision of the Commissioner (C) about incapacity benefit (IB) from 1996. These decisions are binding caselaw in the exactly the same way that decisions of the Upper Tribunal are.

Decisions of the First-tier Tribunal do not constitute caselaw: they do not have to be followed by decision makers in other cases, or by other First-tier Tribunals.

---

Box C
**Where can you look up the law?**

- As a first step, look up a description of the relevant law, for example in CPAG's *Welfare Benefits and Tax Credits Handbook* or Disability Rights UK's *Disability Rights Handbook*. If you have a representative, s/he may have a copy. You may also be able to look at a copy in your local library.

- Next, look at the law itself. Legal references to the law are found, for example, in the footnotes to CPAG's *Welfare Benefits and Tax Credits Handbook*.

- The law can be accessed online. The main official site, the Department for Work and Pensions' so-called 'Blue Volumes', is at www.dwp.gov.uk/publications/specialist-guides/law-volumes/the-law-relating-to-social-security. New legislation appears on www.legislation.gov.uk.

- The law is accompanied by commentary in Sweet and Maxwell's *Social Security Legislation* books and CPAG's *Housing Benefit and Council Tax Reduction Legislation* (the tribunal has copies of these books in the tribunal room). The commentary indicates the key decisions in the caselaw and describes the main points.

- Check for recent caselaw developments using the Upper Tribunal website at www.justice.gov.uk/tribunals/aa (for the decisions themselves), the *Rightsnet* website

---

(www.rightsnet.org.uk) and CPAG's *Welfare Rights Bulletin* (for descriptions of the decisions).

- Other organisations may have useful publications and websites. For example the *Adviser* magazine (published by Citizens Advice) summarises recent caselaw. The Disability Rights UK website (http://disabilityrightsuk.org) has information about benefits for people with illness or disability, including about benefit appeals.

**What law is relevant to your appeal?**

The law that is relevant is that which applies to the 'point of your appeal'. There is more information about this on page 55.

**EXAMPLE**

**The relevant law**

Niall appeals against a decision made before he is transferred to universal credit, that he is not entitled to income-related employment and support allowance because he fails the work capability assessment.

His representative identifies that the 'point of the appeal' is whether Niall should score more points in the mental health assessment and, if not, whether he should still pass the assessment, as not do so would pose a substantial risk to his health.

The relevant law is where the work capability assessment, including the mental health assessment, is set out. For income-related employment and support allowance, that is at Schedule 2 of the Employment and Support Allowance Regulations 2008. Also relevant is the rule about substantial risk, which is set out at regulation 29 of those regulations. (If Niall was appealing about failing the work capability assessment after he had been transferred to universal credit, the relevant law is at Schedules 6 and 8 of the Universal Credit Regulations 2013.)

It is not usually necessary to look up the law about things that are not closely linked to the point of the appeal.

### Does your appeal have complex legal issues?

Usually, appeals do not involve complex legal issues. Most involve just one or two points of law that relate to the point of the appeal, and the tribunal is usually more concerned with facts like how your illness or disability affects you.

However, a few appeals do involve more complex legal points. Examples are where there is a question about whether a particular rule may be in breach of human rights legislation, or whether the law permits a particular regulation to have been made. Sometimes, the caselaw that has developed around a particular rule may be quite complex. Currently, the most common area of social security law that involved complex legal issues is the 'right to reside' test that applies to many benefits and to tax credits.

*What CPAG says*

**Complex legal issues**

If you are not experienced in social security appeals and there is a complex legal issue involved in your appeal, it is particularly advisable to refer the case to a welfare rights adviser or representative, or at least to take further advice from such a person.

CPAG has an advice service for advisers and representatives (but not for people dealing with their own claim; you should first seek help from an adviser or representative at a local advice centre). For details, for advisers in England and Wales see www.cpag.org.uk/advisers, and for those in Scotland see www.cpag.org.uk/content/advice-and-information-advisers.

## 6. How do you gather facts and evidence?

The next step in preparing your appeal is to gather relevant facts and evidence, bearing in mind what you have found out about the relevant law. Exactly what facts and evidence are relevant depends on why you are appealing.

Box D
**Facts and evidence – general tips**

- Do not assume that the decision maker has already gathered all the relevant facts and evidence. For example, s/he may not have contacted your GP or consultant for further evidence.

- There may have been mistakes about some relevant facts, for instance an error in a medical report about how far you can walk. You (or your representative) should point these out to the tribunal – don't leave it to the tribunal to spot it.

- However, do not point out mistakes such as simple spelling mistakes just for the sake of it – always consider whether it is relevant to the point of appeal.

- Allow time to gather facts and evidence; this can be time-consuming, but could be key to winning your appeal.

*What CPAG says*

**Further evidence**

A good representative may be able to help you with gathering facts getting further evidence. For example, s/he may be able to write to your GP or consultant to get a letter to help with your appeal. For more about this and difficulties getting further medical evidence, see Chapter 5.

If you cannot get a representative, use the information in this section to help in gathering facts and evidence.

Further evidence (for example, from your GP) can be very important in winning your appeal. But sometimes it is difficult to get such evidence, and there are increasing reports of such difficulty, such as GPs refusing to supply it. You do not have an automatic right to be given further evidence for your appeal, and you may be charged for it. The tribunal will not get evidence for you, unless (in exceptional cases) it considers that is necessary to make a decision.

## What are the relevant facts?

One of the main jobs of the tribunal is to establish what the relevant facts are. Facts are things like, for example, how far you can walk, how long it takes you to walk a certain distance or complete a certain kind of activity, what kind of help you need with daily activities. In appeals about whether you are living with someone as a couple, facts like whether you share household duties and bills with someone else may be important.

The tribunal expects you (or your representative) to help establish the relevant facts as far as you can. You (or your representative) should point out an errors or things that have been left out to the tribunal. In particular check the following.

- What happened when you claimed: did you represent your facts correctly on the claim form? In a case about illness or disability, do you think the health professional who examined you got all the correct facts?

- Claim forms and medical reports: is there anything there that is relevant but has been overlooked in the decision? Are there important mistakes in the medical report?

- The facts as stated in the decision maker's submission in the appeal papers: are there things there that actually support your appeal? Are there important mistakes?

## What evidence do you need?

There are very few rules about evidence. There is no formal law of evidence at tribunals, so potentially all kinds of evidence (such as oral, written, recorded, video) can be considered.

You are not actually required to gather further evidence to support your appeal. The tribunal can just reconsider the decision on the basis of the evidence is already has. What you say does not have to be supported by other evidence ('corroborated') to be accepted; but a tribunal considers ('weighs') all the evidence on its merits, and is not obliged to adopt one piece of evidence over another. The tribunal can decide that it prefers evidence that contradicts what you say.

However, in practice, most tribunals, as a matter of common sense, do look for further evidence, and getting it will help your case. The basic advice is to get supportive evidence if you can, and where possible send it in to the tribunal in advance.

This is one of the key reasons why an oral hearing, where you attend the tribunal hearing, has a greater chance of success than a 'paper hearing'. In an oral hearing, the tribunal can talk to you and find out more about your abilities and things like what may have gone wrong at the medical.

### EXAMPLES

**Relevant facts and evidence**

The point of Lucy's appeal is to show entitlement to the mobility component of personal independence payment. The relevant facts and evidence are those about Lucy's ability to move around or plan and follow a journey.

The point of Walid's appeal is to show that his tenancy is not 'contrived' and is on a commercial basis for housing benefit. The relevant facts and evidence are things such as an agreement for the tenancy, why the tenancy was created, what the level of rent is and his payment history.

**Can the tribunal direct you to provide further evidence?**

The tribunal can ask or 'direct' you (or your representative) to provide further evidence, but in practice that is not common. It is more common for the tribunal to direct the decision maker to provide further evidence. You can ask that the tribunal direct the decision maker to provide further evidence if you think it essential for a proper reconsideration of the decision under appeal.

*What the law says*

### Tribunal directions about evidence

Tribunals can issue directions about the evidence it requires, the way it is given, whether an oath is required, can exclude evidence not provided as directed and can issue a summons to a witness.

*Rules 15 and 16 Tribunal Procedure (First-tier Tribunal) (Social Entitlement Chamber) Rules*

### EXAMPLE

**Direction to provide medical reports**

Monique is appealing against a decision that she fails the work capability assessment.

In the past she has always passed the work capability assessment, and Monique feels she has not got any better since. However, the Department for Work and Pensions has not included the medical reports from the assessments that she passed. Monique asks the tribunal to direct the decision maker to supply the medical reports from those assessments, as without them there cannot be a proper reconsideration of the decision regarding the most recent one.

### How does the tribunal consider the evidence?

The tribunal considers the evidence by 'weighing' it. It decides how much reliance it can place on a particular piece of evidence and whether (and to what extent) one piece of evidence is to be preferred over another. It can discount a particular piece of evidence entirely. For example, although what you say about your abilities is evidence, a tribunal can discount it completely if it thinks your evidence is improbable or contradictory, or it can prefer other evidence if it considers that evidence is more reliable.

- In appeals where an official medical report is being disputed (such as in a personal independence payment appeal), the tribunal may often attach importance to medical evidence (for example, from a GP or consultant) submitted on your behalf. However, the tribunal should weigh the evidence according to its merits in the particular case, not assume that any one sort of evidence or source of evidence will always be preferable. The tribunal should not assume that the official medical report is the best evidence available, just because it is the official report.

- The tribunal should decide which evidence is the best on the particular facts of the case.

- The tribunal should not assume that evidence is biased – for example, that your GP has supported you simply because you are her/his patient.

### What the law says

**GP's evidence**

A GP is a professional person not forced by anybody to give one answer rather than another, and could say a claimant is exaggerating if he thought that was the case.

*CIB/14442/1996 (decision of the Social Security Commissioner)*

The tribunal can only consider the circumstances that applied at the date of the decision under appeal. That means the date of the original decision that you are unhappy about. It cannot consider changes of circumstance that occur after that date, even if the change was before the date of the 'mandatory reconsideration' of the original decision. So the evidence must be about the circumstances that applied at the time of the decision under appeal. If the evidence is not clearly about those circumstances, the tribunal may decide to give it little weight.

## What the law says

### Changes of circumstance and evidence

The tribunal cannot take into account circumstances after the date of the decision under appeal, but is not limited to evidence that was before the officer who made the decision under appeal or that was in existence at the date of that decision.

*R(DLA) 3/01 (decision of the Social Security Commissioner)*

That does not mean that the evidence itself must have existed at the time, rather that it must be about the circumstances that existed at that time. So, for example, a doctor's letter about your ability to walk should be about your ability to walk at the time of the decision under appeal; it should not matter that the doctor actually wrote the letter after that date.

## What kind of evidence is relevant?

What evidence is important depends on what is actually at issue in your appeal. Bear in mind that the tribunal can consider any sort of evidence. Box E lists examples of evidence commonly in use in appeals.

### Box E
### Evidence commonly used in appeals

- What you say at the oral hearing. This is very important evidence in a successful appeal. If you have a representative, the tribunal does not usually want her/him to give your evidence for you, unless you are unable to do so. However, your representative is allowed to ask you questions.

- A witness attending the oral hearing. This could be, for example, your carer or a relative, or even the person with whom you are alleged to be living with as husband and wife or civil partner.

- Medical evidence such as that from your GP or consultant. This is often important in appeals about illness or disability. For more information about medical evidence, see Chapter 5.

- Evidence showing how variations in your ability due to illness or disability work over time. For example, a 'care diary', showing your daily care needs over a month can be helpful. For more about this, see Chapter 5.

- Non-medical information showing how your illness or disability affects your daily life. Evidence from a social worker or a carer, friend or relative can be helpful supporting evidence.

## 7. How do you write a submission?

The next stage in preparing your appeal is to write a brief 'submission'. This is usually done by your representative, if you have one.

If you do not have a representative, the tribunal does not expect you to write a submission for your own appeal. However, you can still write one for your own case, in which case you may find the advice in this section helpful.

A submission is basically just a setting out of your case, highlighting what you are asking for and how the relevant facts and evidence support that. There is nothing to say that you must have a written submission. It could just be stated verbally at the tribunal hearing. And there is no particular form in which a written submission must be. However, in practice tribunals often find a written submission very helpful, and if you have a representative the tribunal will hope to get a submission from her/him.

Writing a submission and sending it in to the tribunal is a good idea for the following reasons.

- It is a good way for you or your representative, if you have one, to set out ideas for the appeal, so it helps you to clarify your thinking.

- It means you do not have to remember everything at the hearing – you can refer to the submission.

- If the submission is sent in advance, there is a chance that the decision maker may change the decision in your favour without the need for a hearing.

- If the submission is sent in advance, the tribunal will read it before the hearing and it may help influence its thinking.

- Tribunals like written submissions. If you have a representative and s/he has sent in a submission, the tribunal will think that s/he has been helpful and co-operative.

**What should be in a submission?**

There are no specific requirements for the content or layout of a submission. Box F lists the basic principles to be followed.

Box F
**Submissions – basic principles**

- Be brief – no more than a side or two of A4 paper in most cases.

- Set out the information clearly, with headings and numbered paragraphs.

- Identify the decision under appeal and give your details and those of your representative.

- Have a summary of why the appeal has been made and what decision is being sought.

- Set out relevant facts and evidence. This need not be all the facts that have been gathered, just those relevant to the point of the appeal.

- Set out reasons why your appeal should succeed (these are your 'representations').

- Briefly mention any law or caselaw that is especially important in your case. In many cases there is nothing to point out, as the tribunal knows the basic rules that should apply. However, if you or your representative have identified a particular piece of caselaw that is very relevant to the facts of you case, then it can be mentioned. Reference to the caselaw commentary in the *Social Security Legislation* law volumes published by Sweet and Maxwell is also helpful – but always make sure you or your representative read a full copy of any piece of caselaw before it is used in a submission. Send a copy of the caselaw with your submission in advance if possible.

- If a particular part of the decision is not being challenged (such as some points awarded in the work capability assessment), say so.

- You can make more than one argument. For example, you can ask that if the tribunal does not accept one descriptor in the work capability assessment or the test for personal independence payment, then it considers an alternative one instead.

- Point out the strengths of your appeal – for example, where the evidence supports what you say. Don't leave it up to the tribunal to spot such things.

- Point out omissions or mistakes in the submission made by the decision maker, as well as in any official evidence such as the official medical report. This can include, where relevant, things like the fact that variations in your ability were not fully explored at the official medical.

- If pointing out things in the appeal papers, refer to the page number where they are located.

### What might a written submission look like?

You do not have to write a submission in a particular way. If you have a representative, s/he may have developed her/his own preferred style and have a basic 'skeleton' submission which can be adapted to the facts of your case. However, the submission set out below is recommended as a basic structure and content.

## Appeal submission

Rhian Evans is appealing against a decision (confirmed in a mandatory reconsideration notice) that she does not have limited capability for work and so is not entitled to employment and support allowance. This is an example of a submission written by Rhian's representative. The representative has been able to get a supportive letter from the GP.

### Submission

**Claimant:** Ms Rhian Evans [details of Rhian's address, telephone number and national insurance number]

**Tribunal:** [details of the tribunal reference number, hearing date and venue if possible]

**Representative:** [name and work address of representative, including telephone number]

**Date of decision under appeal:** 3 November 2013

**Date of mandatory reconsideration notice:** 20 November 2013

### 1. Summary

Ms Evans appeals against the decision dated 3 November 2013 that she does not have limited capability for work and is therefore not entitled to employment and support allowance. The decision was confirmed in a mandatory reconsideration notice dated 20 November 2013.

She submits that she does have limited capability for work as she scores sufficient points under the work capability assessment to satisfy the assessment.

Ms Evans submits that the following descriptors and points should apply, so that her points score is 18 and above the threshold:

- cannot repeatedly mobilise 100 metres within a reasonable timescale because of significant discomfort or exhaustion (descriptor 1(c)(ii), 9 points)

- cannot cope with minor planned change (such as a pre-arranged change to the routine time scheduled for a lunch break), to the extent that overall day-to-day life is made significantly more difficult (descriptor 14(b), 9 points)

In the event of the tribunal considering that descriptor 14(b) does not apply, it is invited also to consider whether descriptor 14(c) (cannot cope with minor unplanned change, 6 points) applies in the alternative.

If the tribunal is unable to find that Ms Evans scores sufficient points, it is requested to consider whether she should nevertheless be treated as having limited capability for work, on the basis that not to do so would pose a substantial risk to her health (regulation 29 Employment and Support Allowance Regulations 2008).

## 2. Facts and evidence

2.1 Ms Evans suffers from a chronic back condition and depression, for which she is treated by her GP – see the letter from her GP, Dr Smith, at page 40 of the appeal papers. These conditions affect her daily life to a considerable extent.

The back condition means:

- it is painful for her to bend and straighten up

- she has difficulty with walking, to the extent that although she may be able to walk 100 metres once, she could not do so again for a long time (3–4 hours, and frequently longer) because of the pain that she is in

2.2 Her ability to repeatedly mobilise seems not to have been considered in detail by the examining healthcare professional (pages 30–35). Ms Evans says that he seemed only to be concerned with her walking ability at its very best and did not ask about her ability to repeat this. Her GP confirms that she is likely to have this sort of problem with her walking, and that she would be unable to propel herself in a manual wheelchair (page 40).

2.3 Ms Evans also suffers from anxiety and depression which is only moderately well controlled by medication (letter from Dr Smith, page 40). One of the effects of the depression is that she has great difficulty coping with minor changes to her daily routine, which tend to upset her to the extent that managing day-to-day life is much more difficult for her.

Ms Evans submits that this applies both to planned and unplanned changes in her daily routine. For example, she becomes greatly distressed by alterations to travel arrangments and her usual shopping routine. Ms Evans did state on her ESA50 questionnaire (page 35) that she often gets upset with such changes to her daily routine.

This is supported by her GP (page 40). Ms Evans says that the examining healthcare professional did not ask her many questions about this at the medical, and thinks therefore that he did not fully understand how the problem affects her.

### 3. Representations

3.1 It is submitted this appeal is well supported by the evidence from Ms Evans and her GP, who has treated her for three years and knows her well. It is submitted that this should be preferred to the official medical report, as based on longer knowledge of her and a better understanding of her limitations. It is submitted that the official medical is partly inaccurate as the examining healthcare professional did not properly explore the variability in Ms Evans's walking ability or the effects of her anxiety and depression.

3.2 It is submitted that the evidence shows that due to her inability to walk repeatedly and her inability to use a manual wheelchair, Ms Evans satisfies descriptor 1(c)(ii). This descriptor scores 9 points. It is submitted that this descriptor applies as a person without restriction would be able to mobilise 100 metres several times a day.

3.3 It is also submitted that due to her anxiety and depression and in particular inability to cope with minor changes, Ms Evans satisfies descriptor 14(b). This descriptor scores 9 points. It is submitted that this descriptor applies given the extent of distress caused to her by changes to everyday things like travel arrangements and shopping plans.

3.4 If the tribunal does not accept that this applies, it is submitted that for the same reasons descriptor 14(c) applies for inability to cope with minor unplanned change (6 points).

3.5. If the tribunal is unable to find that Ms Evans scores sufficient points, it is submitted that she should be treated as having limited capability for work on the basis that there will be a substantial risk to her health if she is not. It is submitted that this arises from the risk that her anxiety and depression will be substantially worsened by the demands of having to respond to changes in her daily routine occasioned by having to cope with the demands of work, such as travel difficulties and having to cope with even minor changes in her daily work routine.

3.6 It is not submitted that Ms Evans is in the support group on the basis of having limited capability for work-related activity.

## 4. Caselaw

No caselaw is submitted as especially relevant to this case.

### Further information

If you do not have a representative, see CPAG's appeals toolkit (www.cpag.org.uk/appeals-toolkit) for help with preparing your appeal yourself.

# Chapter 5
# Illness and disability appeals

This chapter covers:

1. What problems can occur with these appeals?

2. Problems around medical evidence

3. What the tribunal can do

4. Increasing your chances of winning your appeal

## What you need to know

- Appeals about illness and disability are basically like any other appeal; however particular problems sometimes apply in these appeals. A good representative will be able to help you deal with them.

- Some problems concern getting further medical evidence, and where the tribunal may want to give little weight to such evidence.

- The tribunal cannot take into account changes in your circumstances after you have appealed, including where your condition has worsened.

- The tribunal can use evidence from another of your benefit claims. It can also decide to make a decision that is actually less favourable to you than the one you appealed against.

- In appeals about the work capability assessment, understanding of the 'exceptional circumstances' rules can be important; in disability appeals, a care/mobility diary is often very helpful additional evidence.

## 1. What problems can occur with these appeals?

Many appeals are about illness or about disability. In particular, many appeals are about the work capability assessment for employment and support allowance and universal credit (see Box A), and about the disability tests for personal independence payment and disability living allowance.

> Box A
> **The work capability assessment**
>
> The work capability assessment is the test used to decide whether you have 'limited capability for work' – ie, whether you are currently unable to work. The test applies to entitlement to employment and support allowance, and also whether or not you get additional universal credit if you or your partner are ill or disabled. The assessment normally involves your filling in a questionnaire and attending a medical examination.
>
> The work capability assessment also tests whether you have 'limited capability for work-related activity'. This is to identify if your illness or disability is so serious that you should not be expected to plan for returning to work. If you are assessed as having limited capability for work-related activity, you are placed in the 'support group' for employment and support allowance.

If your appeal is about illness or disability, the main rules about the way the tribunal deals with your appeal are the same as for any other appeal. However, there are some problems that sometimes arise in these appeals. These include:

- getting medical evidence – where your doctor refuses to supply further evidence or wants to charge for supplying it
- considering medical evidence – where the tribunal wants to automatically prefer the official medical report, or give the medical evidence from your doctor little weight
- the tribunal cannot take into account changes in your circumstances while you are waiting for your appeal to be heard – in particular, where your condition gets worse

- there may be evidence in the appeal papers from another of your benefit claims – for instance, evidence from your personal independence payment claim when considering your appeal about the work capability assessment
- the tribunal may want to make a decision that is actually less favourable to you than the one you appealed against

## 2. Problems around medical evidence

*What CPAG says*

**Getting further evidence**

You are not actually required to get further medical evidence, and there is no rule that says you must be given it if you ask for it. But, in practice, it is strongly advisable to get further medical evidence if you can, especially in appeals about illness or disability. Although the tribunal has knowledge of medical matters and disability, it does not conduct a medical examination (unless your appeal is about industrial injuries disablement benefit). The appeal papers very often contain the official medical report so, unless you provide further evidence, there can sometimes seem to be an imbalance in the evidence that is available to the tribunal. Although further medical evidence is not essential to win your appeal, it is often important.

A good representative may be able to help you get further medical evidence – for example, by writing to your doctor.

The further medical evidence is often a supportive letter from a doctor (a GP or consultant). Other sources of supportive medical evidence include:

- occupational therapists
- physiotherapists
- clinical psychologists
- community psychiatric nurses

- existing medical evidence – for instance, previous ESA85 medical reports in which you passed the work capability assessment

Sometimes, evidence from people who are not medically qualified may also be relevant. Potential sources of such evidence include:

- social workers
- support workers
- care workers

## Has your doctor refused to supply medical evidence?

Your doctor is under no obligation to provide you with medical evidence for your appeal. You (or your representative) can ask the doctor for evidence but s/he does not have to supply it. Doctors are required to supply information to the decision maker where requested, but not to you or your representative.

In practice, workload and other pressures (including information from the Department for Work and Pensions (DWP) emphasising that they have no obligation to supply evidence to claimants) has led to increasing numbers of doctors, especially GPs, refusing to supply medical evidence. It is very important to remember that your doctor is not obliged to supply evidence to you, and that s/he very probably has a heavy workload.

If your doctor refuses to supply evidence to you, you can:

- try to persuade your doctor to provide the evidence – see Box B
- find other medical evidence to support your appeal – see Box C

Box B
**Persuading your doctor to provide evidence**

- Ensure that your doctor knows that the very point of an appeal is because something may have gone wrong with the official medical assessment – that the job of the tribunal includes considering the accuracy of the official medical report.

- Emphasise that it is a short letter that is required rather than a lengthy medical report.

- Point out that your doctor may have much better knowledge of you than the examining doctor, who has only examined you once.

- Ensure that your doctor knows that many appeals are successful – for example, about 43 per cent of employment and support allowance appeals against work capability assessment failures are successful, with higher rates of success at oral hearings.

- Your representative can consider liaising with local doctors, such as arranging meetings at local medical centres to explain the importance of their support; this might be done in collaboration with people working on appeals in other organisations. In response to such liaison, some GPs have reduced their charges, or dropped them altogether.

- If your doctor does supply supportive evidence, remember to thank her/him and report the outcome of the appeal.

If your doctor cannot be persuaded to supply further medical evidence, there may be other medical evidence already in existence. Some of this may actually be in the appeal papers. For example, the official medical report may say some things in your favour. Alternatively, there may be relevant medical evidence that was produced about matters other than your claim for benefit. Such evidence is not usually as relevant for your appeal as a letter from your doctor, but may still be helpful.

Box C
**Finding other medical evidence**

- Ask your doctor for a copy of your records that are held electronically. You may be charged for this.

- Is there other medical evidence in the appeal papers that supports your appeal? For example, a copy of a previous ESA85 medical report in which you passed work capability assessment.

- If your appeal is about the work capability assessment, if there is a previous ESA85 medical report that is still relevant (because your condition has not changed) but it is not in the appeal papers, the DWP can be directed by the tribunal to include it, as otherwise the hearing may not be fair.

- Is there a medical report produced for another benefit that you have claimed that may be relevant? In particular, medical reports from personal independence payment or disability living allowance claims may be used as evidence in employment and support allowance appeals, and vice versa, although only where relevant, and even then with considerable care, bearing in mind that the benefits have different rules.

- Do you have an occupational therapy assessment, or a social worker's report that may be helpful?

- The tribunal could get further medical evidence for use in your appeal, if it considers that is necessary for its decision. However, it is rare for a tribunal to do this as it usually has the medical evidence already. If it does get further medical evidence, this is not necessarily from your doctor – it could be from the DWP. You are not charged for this.

### Does your doctor want to charge?

Your doctor may be willing to provide you with further medical evidence, but may wish to charge you (or your representative) for it. There is no rule preventing that, or limiting the amount that your doctor can charge. In practice, GPs may often charge up to £100, and a consultant even more. You may pay the charge if you are able and willing to do so. It is very unlikely that your representative will be able to pay for you.

If you cannot afford to pay:

- emphasise to the doctor that you have been refused benefit and cannot afford to pay

- make it clear that your representative is unable to pay
- emphasise that it is only a short letter, not a lengthy medical report, that is required
- in Scotland (but not England or Wales), Legal Aid (via advice and assistance) may be able to pay for the evidence, if you are eligible – your representative may be able to help you apply
- your representative could consider liaising with your GP

**How does the tribunal consider the medical evidence?**

There are very few rules on how the tribunal must consider (or 'weigh') medical evidence. Many of the most important details on the weighing process come from caselaw. The tribunal should make up its own mind about what should apply. The formal law of evidence does not apply to the tribunal, and it should weigh each piece of evidence on its own merits, without assuming that one sort of evidence is automatically better than another. For example, a very short piece of evidence from a doctor that is general in nature may well be given less weight by the tribunal than a detailed medical report that focuses specifically on the issues.

Caselaw has established that it is incorrect to assume that the official medical report is automatically correct. Neither should the tribunal make *assumptions*, such as that your doctor is acting under pressure from you; although, if the tribunal is justified in deciding that, it needs to have specific reasons based on the facts of your case.

If you think the tribunal may be taking an incorrect approach to weighing, it could be asked to clarify why it is taking such an approach. The tribunal should be aware of the relevant caselaw, however if necessary, it could be referred to some of the caselaw in Box D. Ultimately, a tribunal decision that is based on such an approach may contain an error of law and be challenged on a further appeal to the Upper Tribunal.

## Box D
### Weighing medical evidence – caselaw examples

Medical evidence in the form of opinion only (where the reasons for it are not apparent) may be given little weight.
*CDLA/2961/2004; CDLA/1572/2005 (decisions of the Social Security Commissioners)*

Holding that the official medical report must automatically be preferred to that of the claimant would fly in the face of the obligation of the tribunal to consider all of the evidence.
In incapacity and disability cases, the appeal is in effect against the official medical report, and to say that is automatically to be preferred is inconsistent with the impartiality of the tribunal.
*R(DLA) 3/99; CIB/3074/2003 (decisions of the Social Security Commissioner)*

The tribunal may prefer the evidence of a GP who has treated the claimant over many years; in others it may prefer the evidence of a specialist who is skilled in the condition from which the claimant suffers. They may attach little weight to a terse certificate from a GP.
*R(M) 1/93 (a decision of the Social Security Commissioner)*

Tribunals should not give 'formulaic' reasons for endorsing the official medical report – ie, merely on the basis that it is 'expert' and by someone trained in applying the test.
*AG v Secretary of State for Work and Pensions [2009] UKUT 127 (AAC) (a decision of the Upper Tribunal)*

A GP is a professional person not forced by anybody to give one answer rather than another; the tribunal should not assume that the claimant is putting words in the GP's mouth.
The tribunal should not say that the GP is likely to be under pressure from the claimant unless there is specific evidence about that.
*CIB/14442/1996; CDLA/2277/2005 (decisions of the Social Security Commissioners)*

The GP's letter included his express views and the tribunal should not have implied that the doctor had merely acted as a cipher for what the claimant said; although GP reports were often limited in the relevant information they provide, their limitations do not mean that they are valueless; tribunals must balance each report's values and limitations.

*HL v Secretary of State for Work and Pensions (DLA) [2011] UKUT 183 (AAC) (a decision of the Upper Tribunal)*

To be given weight by the tribunal, your medical evidence should focus on what is relevant to your appeal. For example, a diagnosis and list of treatment is less useful than a letter which states how you are affected by your condition, ideally with reference to the point of the appeal and the descriptors and points being argued for. However, it is best to make it clear that the doctor is being asked to express her/his own opinion. You should not attempt to pressurise the doctor into giving the evidence that you want.

---

**Box E**

**Getting good medical evidence**

- Ask for a short letter focusing on the point of the appeal (for example, the descriptors and points being argued for) rather than more general information.
- Ask 'open' questions asking for the doctor's own view, rather than 'closed' or leading questions simply asking the doctor to agree with what you say, or giving her/him the answer that you want. An example of an open question is, 'the tribunal will be considering whether the following statements can be applied, can you comment'; an example of a closed or leading question is, 'can you confirm that I cannot walk more than 20 metres'.
- Ask for brief reasons for the opinions given – if the evidence is in the form of *opinion* only, it may be given less weight.
- Ensure the evidence relates to your abilities at the time of the original decision under appeal – the tribunal cannot take account of changes since that date, even if the change was before the date of the 'mandatory reconsideration' of the decision (it does not matter, however, that the evidence itself was produced at a later date).

- If your representative is requesting the evidence for your, s/he should ensure that there is a form of authority giving your permission for the doctor to supply the evidence.
- When sending medical evidence to the tribunal, ensure that the letter asking for the evidence is also included, so that the tribunal can see what you said to the doctor.

## EXAMPLE

### Letter seeking medical evidence

This letter is a letter from a representative who is helping Rhian Evans with her appeal.

Dear Dr Smith,

**Re: Rhian Evans, 12 Bevan Road, Splott, Cardiff**

**Date of birth: 3/3/70**

We are writing on behalf of the above who we understand is your patient. We include a form of authority from her.

Following a medical assessment on behalf of the Department for Work and Pensions, Ms Evans has been refused entitlement to employment and support allowance, as she is not considered to have limited capability for work. She has, with our assistance, appealed against that decision to an independent tribunal. The tribunal will reconsider the decision, and has the power to uphold it or decide that it should be changed. We are writing on behalf of Ms Evans to ask if you could provide a short letter to assist with that.

We appreciate that your time is limited. However, the tribunal will find a short letter focused on the relevant questions more helpful that a longer medical report.

The tribunal will be considering whether the following statements, taken from the official work capability assessment, may be applied to Ms Evans as at the date of the decision on 1

June 2013 (the tribunal may not take into account any changes in her condition after that date).

We would be grateful if you could comment as to whether you agree or disagree that these statements may be applied to Ms Evans, with a brief indication of your reasons, or are instead unable to comment. A brief statement of any medication and treatment she has would also be helpful.

1. Cannot repeatedly mobilise (including using a walking stick, manual wheelchair or other aid which is normally, or could normally be, used) 100 metres within a reasonable timescale because of significant discomfort or exhaustion.

2. Cannot cope with minor planned change (such as a pre-arranged change to the routine time schedule for a lunch break), to the extent that overall day-to-day life is made significantly more difficult.

Please be advised that as Ms Evans is on a very low income and our organisation has very limited funds, neither she nor ourselves would be able to meet a charge for supply of the letter. If you do propose to charge, please contact us before proceeding.

Thanking you in advance for your assistance.

Yours sincerely [etc]

## 3. What the tribunal can do

### Can the tribunal take changes in your circumstances into account?

The basic rule is that a tribunal cannot take into account a change in your circumstances that occurs after the date of the decision that is under appeal. The decision under appeal is the original decision – for example, that you failed the work capability assessment. This applies even if the change in your circumstance occurred after the date of that decision, but before the date of the 'mandatory reconsideration' of the decision.

Because of this, a change that occurs while you are waiting for your appeal to be heard cannot be considered by the tribunal. There are two main consequences of this for winning your appeal.

- Any evidence produced for your appeal should refer (where this is not already obvious) to your condition as at the date of the decision under appeal. Where this is not possible, it may be possible to argue that that does not matter – for example, where your condition has been the same for some time and is clearly not likely to vary much over time. Remember, however, that it is only a *change of circumstance* that cannot be taken into account by the tribunal. The tribunal is not barred from taking into account *evidence* produced after the decision.

- Any significant change in your condition *after the date of the decision under appeal* cannot affect the outcome of the appeal, as the tribunal cannot take it into account. This applies even if you get much worse while you are waiting for your appeal to be heard, something that in practice is not uncommon, as it can take several weeks or months before the appeal is heard.

If your condition changes while you are waiting for your appeal to be heard, get advice about the consequences for your benefit entitlement, as, depending on the facts of your case, the situation can be complex.

If you have some award of benefit, there is an obligation on you to report any change of circumstance that you might reasonably be expected to know might affect your benefit award. This rule is only likely to be important where you actually have an *improvement* in your condition that might affect your current award of benefit while you are waiting for your appeal to be heard, such as where you have been awarded the mobility component of personal independence payment, but your walking improves. So if your condition improves in a way that might affect your benefit, you must report that.

Much more common is the situation where your condition gets *worse* while you are waiting for your appeal to be heard. Given that the tribunal cannot take the change into account, what to do in such situations is not straightforward. The choice is basically between:

- reporting the change and giving rise to another decision which you might need to appeal against
- waiting until the tribunal has made its decision, but possibly missing out on some arrears
- reporting the change but asking the decision maker not to make a decision until the tribunal has decided your appeal

The more serious the worsening in your condition, the greater the case for reporting it. Remember the following general points.

- In a limited capability for work appeal, reporting a change in circumstance may lead to the work capability assessment being carried out again. Your appeal against the original decision will go ahead whatever the outcome of that assessment. But if the second work capability assessment is also failed, then even if your appeal is successful, the decision maker may stop your entitlement continuing as a result. In that case, you need to make another appeal against the decision about the second failed work capability assessment (after you have had a mandatory reconsideration).

- If on the other hand, if you have a second work capability assessment and you pass, it may be that the increase in your benefit entitlement can start straight away, with the tribunal considering only the period between the original decision that is under appeal and the start of entitlement from the second work capability assessment.

- In a personal independence payment or disability living allowance appeal, if you were refused benefit completely in the original decision, you could make a new claim while the appeal is pending. Or, if you were awarded some of a benefit, then a request for that to be looked at again could be made. In either case, you usually get a new (a second) decision and the tribunal then considers only the period between your first and second decisions. If you are also unhappy with the second decision, you need to make another appeal against that (after a mandatory reconsideration).

## Can the tribunal use evidence from another of your benefit claims?

*What the law says*

### Evidence about another benefit

A tribunal can consider medical evidence from an appeal about another benefit, but should do so carefully and bear in mind that different legal tests are involved.

*LD v Secretary of State for Work and Pensions [2009] UKUT 208 (AAC); DK v Secretary of State for Work and Pensions (DLA) [2012] UKUT 254 (decisions of the Upper Tribunal)*

Because the tribunal can take into account any evidence that is relevant, it can sometimes take into account evidence from another of your claims or appeals. This is especially likely where the appeal papers contain evidence from another of your claims or appeals.

It is not uncommon for the same person to have appeals about both the work capability assessment and disability at the same time. Your appeals should be heard completely separately, but evidence from one appeal can be used in the other. The tribunal may consider such evidence relevant – for example, if it concerns your disability and how it affects you, some issues (such as your ability to walk) may be common to both appeals. It should ensure that you (and any other party to the appeal) have proper access to such evidence and are able to comment on it.

*What the law says*

### Appeals about more than one benefit

Tribunals hearing limited capability for work and personal independence payment/disability living allowance appeals should be heard in completely separate sessions by completely differently composed tribunals.

*MB and others v Secretary of State for Work and Pensions (ESA and DLA) [2013] UKUT 111 (AAC) (a decision of the Upper Tribunal)*

Both your appeals must be considered at separate sessions and by differently made up tribunals. Ideally you and your representative need to attend both hearings. As the tribunals are completely separate, it is possible that although one tribunal takes a particular approach or makes a particular finding, the other tribunal may do differently.

Box F
**Appeals about more than one benefit – tactics**

• Consider whether evidence from the other appeal is useful – for example, is it a potential source of supportive medical evidence? If so, what are its strengths and why should the tribunal give weight to it? If you want the evidence from the other appeal to be considered, you should submit it to the tribunal.

• Are there weaknesses in the evidence from the other appeal – do you feel that the medical in the other claim was of poor quality for some reason?

• Remember that the different appeals concern different legal tests and, if necessary, emphasise that to the tribunal – for example, the mobility-related test for personal independence payment involves being able to stand, and uses different distances than that in the work capability assessment.

**Can the tribunal make a less favourable decision?**

The tribunal has the power to make a decision that is actually less favourable to you than the one you appealed against. Because the tribunal holds the power to make a complete reconsideration of the decision under appeal, it can make whatever decision the decision maker *could* have made. This is the case even if you have not specifically appealed against all parts of the decision. The tribunal does not have to look at these unappealed parts of the decision; but it *can* if it thinks that those parts of the decision may be wrong.

The tribunal either upholds the decision under appeal, or changes it so as to award benefit. However, in a few cases, where the decision under appeal includes some award of benefit, the tribunal can not only refuse the appeal but can also change the decision so as to *reduce or remove* your entitlement.

The making of a less favourable decision is most likely in some disability living allowance appeals and personal independence payment appeals. This is because there are a number of things about entitlement included in the decision: whether there is entitlement to one or both components, what rate they are awarded at and for how long. So an appeal about one aspect of the decision in fact allows the other aspects to be considered too.

---

**EXAMPLE**

**Less favourable decision**

Jalal receives a decision that he is entitled to the daily living component of personal independence payment (at the standard rate), but he is not entitled to the mobility component. Jalal thinks he should get the mobility component too and appeals.

However, after considering the evidence, the tribunal thinks that it may not only refuse his appeal about the mobility component, but also alter the decision so as to remove his entitlement to the daily living component.

The tribunal warns Jalal that it is considering this. If he decides to continue with the appeal, the tribunal has the power to take away the daily living component as well as to refuse the mobility component.

---

In theory at least, something similar could happen in an appeal about the work capability assessment – for example, where you have appealed because you think you should be placed in the support group, and the tribunal wants not only to refuse that appeal but also to reconsider whether you have limited capability for work – so as to reconsider whether you satisfy the work capability assessment at all. That could result in the loss of benefit altogether.

Again, this is because both are elements of the same decision. In practice, however, this is uncommon.

It is more common for a tribunal that allows an appeal about limited capability for work (so that the work capability assessment is passed) to go on to consider whether you should be put in the support group (see Box A). The Department for Work and Pensions normally requests that the tribunal does this, but if you want to be sure that the tribunal does so, you should also request this.

---

Box G
**Avoiding a less favourable decision – tactics**

- Is there an element of the decision on your claim which could be the subject of a less favourable decision? For example, is there an award of a personal independence payment component that you are happy with and have not appealed about, but that may not be very secure? If so, consider whether continuing the appeal is advisable. Remember that the tribunal can look at all elements of the appeal and may want to consider unappealed parts of the decision that do not look very secure.

- If the tribunal indicates that it wishes to consider an unappealed part of the decision, it should let you know and allow you at least a brief adjournment. It may offer you the opportunity of a longer adjournment to consider the unappealed part of the decision, or allow you to withdraw your appeal. If you have a representative, the tribunal expects her/him to help you decide what to do.

- An indication from the tribunal that it wants to do this in your appeal, rather than a mere general statement, is a strong indication that it is considering a less favourable decision. If you are not sure what the tribunal means, ask the judge to clarify if the tribunal is likely to consider an unappealed part of the decision.

- Be careful about declining an offer of an adjournment – if you do this but then later wish to argue that the tribunal should have granted one then it will be very difficult to succeed.

---

- If you wish to get further evidence about the unappealed part of the decision, or want more time to consider the evidence about that, the tribunal should allow an adjournment for that – but is not obliged to.

- In appeals about limited capability for work, a tribunal that allows the appeal should go on to consider whether or not you are in the support group. But if you want to be sure that the tribunal does this, ask it to do so.

## 4. Increasing your chances of winning your appeal

Appeals about illness or disability are in many ways no different from any other appeal. So having the following are, as in any appeal, very important:

- an oral hearing of the appeal attended by you and ideally your representative
- evidence that supports your appeal, in particular supportive medical evidence such as a letter from your GP or consultant

There are other things that you can do that may increase your chances of winning your appeal. One applies where you have an appeal about the work capability assessment; the other applies where you have an appeal about disability.

### Work capability assessment appeals

In work capability assessment appeals, an understanding of the 'substantial risk' rules can be a potential additional route to a successful appeal. However, they are sometimes overlooked.

It is a good idea to consider whether there is an argument that the substantial risk rules should apply, even where arguments are also being made that points should apply. You can argue both that you should score enough points and that a substantial risk applies if you do not score enough points.

**What the law says**

### The substantial risk rules

If you do not score enough points to win your appeal, you should still do so if otherwise there would be a 'substantial risk' to your physical or mental health, or to someone else's physical or mental health, unless that risk could be avoided by reasonable adjustments.

The 'substantial risk' rules apply both in the assessment of limited capability for work (about whether you pass the work capability assessment at all) and in the assessment of 'limited capability for work-related activity' (about whether or not you are placed in the support group).

*Regulations 29 and 35 The Employment and Support Allowance Regulations 2008; Schedule 8 paragraph 4 and Schedule 9 paragraph 4 The Universal Credit Regulations 2013; regulations 25 and 31 The Employment and Support Allowance Regulations 2013*

The substantial risk could be from doing the sort of work or (in limited capability for work-related activity cases) the sort of work-related activity that you may be expected to do. The tribunal does not need to consider actual job descriptions or a theoretical jobseeker's agreement, just the kind of work that you might be able to do. The risk can include things like risks arising from travelling to or from work as well as factors like, in mental health cases, anxiety or depression caused by the need to look for work.

**What the law says**

### Substantial risk

In a case about limited capability for work, the tribunal should, when considering substantial risk, assess the range or type of work which a claimant is capable of performing, in assessing the risk to her/himself or to others. That can include the journey to or from work.

*Charlton v Secretary of State for Work and Pensions [2009] EWCA Civ 42; R(IB) 2/09 (a decision of the Court of Appeal)*

In appeals about whether or not you are in the support group, there is often little information in the decision about the kind of work-related activity the decision maker thinks you could do. You could ask the tribunal to direct the decision maker to provide further information about this, as in some cases without such information it can be difficult to show that there is a 'substantial risk' from such activity, and so it is difficult for the tribunal to reconsider the decision properly.

### EXAMPLE

**Substantial risk**

Eva appeals against a decision that she fails the work capability assessment and so is not entitled to employment and support allowance. She suffers from anxiety and depression and has problems coping with change and with social situations. These have been severe enough for her to have harmed herself on occasion.

The tribunal allows Eva's appeal so that she is found to have limited capability for work and so satisfies the work capability assessment. Although the tribunal did not score her enough points to pass the assessment, it decides on the evidence that if she did not do so, there would be a substantial risk to her health due to the pressures of a working environment, how that would affect her mental health and how that may cause her to harm herself.

## Disability appeals

In appeals about personal independence payment, disability living allowance and attendance allowance in particular, a care/mobility diary can be a very helpful source of additional evidence, especially if there are significant fluctuations in your condition, so that you tend to have good and bad periods.

For personal independence payment, there are rules about a descriptor from the disability test needing to apply for more than 50 per cent of the days of the one-year period taken into account when deciding entitlement. For disability living allowance or attendance allowance, there is no such specific rule but, in general, the test considers whrther the disability test is satisfied for most of the time. Keeping a care/mobility diary, in which you record the level and frequency of your care needs or your walking ability over a period of time, can help to show whether the test is satisfied. When recording your walking ability, try to indicate not only how far you can walk, but other relevant things such as whether you are using an aid (such as a walking stick), how long it takes you to walk as far as you do, and whether you need to stop because of discomfort or breathlessness.

There is no particular form in which your diary should be kept but be as clear and as accurate as possible. A page for each day is a way of keeping the information clear. Ideally, keep your diary over a period of time which most accurately reflects fluctuations in your condition. So if you tend to have good days and bad days, a period of a few weeks is probably enough; but if you tend to have good weeks and bad weeks, then you may need to keep it for a month or more to get the most helpful diary.

If your condition has significantly changed since the date of the decision under appeal, a note should be included explaining how.

### Further information

An example of a care diary to help with a claim for disability living allowance for a child, drawn up by the Department for Work and Pensions, is available at www.dwp.gov.uk/advisers/claimforms/dla1a_child_print.pdf. Another example is in Disability Rights UK's *Disability Rights Handbook*.
CPAG's *Personal Independence Payment – what you need to know* outlines the assessment criteria used for personal independence payment, including the activities you are tested against and the points you must score to qualify for an award.

# Chapter 6
# The appeal hearing

This chapter covers:

1. What happens before the hearing?

2. What happens at the hearing?

3. What happens after the decision is made?

## What you need to know

- HM Courts and Tribunals Service handles social security appeals. It is important to respond to queries you get about your appeal, as otherwise the appeal may be cancelled (known as 'struck out').

- The appeal is considered either at an oral hearing where you and ideally your representative attend, or just by the tribunal looking at the appeal papers. You are more likely to win your appeal by attending an oral hearing.

- An oral hearing may be recorded.

- Oral hearings can be postponed or adjourned, but there is no legal right to this.

- Hearings do not have precise rules about how they are run, except an overall requirement to be fair.

- Hearings usually consist of short introductions, a summary of the case and then direct questioning by the tribunal.

- Most decisions are given on the same day as the hearing, but may be given later in writing.

## 1. What happens before the hearing?

After you have made your appeal, there are a number of steps before your case is heard by the tribunal.

### After your appeal has been received

#### Most benefits

In most benefit cases where the decision on your claim was made on or after 28 October 2013, you can appeal after you have had the decision looked at again and a decision on that issued (a 'mandatory reconsideration') by the decision maker. In such cases, you send your appeal directly to HM Courts and Tribunals Service.

After HM Courts and Tribunals Service has received your appeal, it checks it to make sure that it is valid. If it thinks there are any problems that need to be rectified, it returns the appeal for you to correct. For example, it may ask you to add your reasons for the appeal. Do not ignore this request. If you do, there is a risk that the appeal will be cancelled ('struck out'). If your appeal is considered valid, or if HM Courts and Tribunals Service thinks that any problems with it can be ignored (or 'waived'), it sends an acknowledgement of this to you. This includes the contact details and telephone number of the office that handles your appeal. An enquiry form may also be included if more details are needed about your availability or requirements for the appeal, such as clarification about whether you want an oral hearing, details of your representative, or whether you need an interpreter. In particular, if a hearing date has been set and that is not suitable for either you or your representative, contact the clerk to the tribunal as soon as possible, explain the situation and request an alternative date. It is strongly advisable to put this request in writing and well in advance, although the request can be renewed on the day of the hearing. If your representative is unable to attend, before an alternative date is considered, the tribunal expects there to be a good reason and there to be no alternative representative available.

A copy of your appeal is sent to the decision maker at the Department for Work and Pensions (DWP). S/he prepares a 'response' to the appeal explaining how the decision was made. The decision maker must do this as soon as reasonably practical. In appeals about universal credit and personal independence payment, the DWP says that this will be done within 28 days, and that the target will apply to other benefit appeals from October 2014 (but note that the target is not actually part of the law).

The decision maker's response is sent as a bundle of appeal papers, both to the HM Courts and Tribunals Service and to you. If you have notified that you have a representative, s/he should be sent the appeal papers – check with her/him though, as this sometimes does not happen. The decision maker's response must include:

- the decision that is being appealed against
- copies of the relevant documents, such as claim forms and official medical reports
- a summary of the relevant facts and the decision maker's reasons for making the decision
- a copy of the appeal form or letter

You or your representative can send in further documents and make a written submission as a reply to the decision maker's response. The official time limit for doing this is within one month of the date on which the decision maker's response was sent, although, in practice, the tribunal may decide to ignore (or 'waive') that time limit, especially if it was not possible to send the material earlier.

### Housing benefit and other benefit cases

For all appeals about housing benefit (or about any other benefit case where a need for a mandatory reconsideration has not been notified), the appeal can be made directly against the original decision, so a 'mandatory reconsideration' is not required. From 28 October 2013 this is likely to apply only to housing benefit decisions, and (probably until April 2014) to tax credits, child benefit and guardian's allowance decisions.

In such cases, the appeal is sent directly to the decision maker rather than to HM Courts and Tribunals Service. So in a housing benefit case, your appeal is sent to the decision maker at the local authority;

in a child benefit case, it is sent to the decision maker at HM Revenue and Customs.

The decision maker prepares a response to the appeal, and sends it to HM Courts and Tribunals Service and to you. If the appeal is late and the decision maker objects to it going ahead, s/he should refer it to HM Courts and Tribunals Service immediately.

HM Courts and Tribunals Service then takes over the handling of the appeal, and sends you an enquiry form asking about your availability, whether you want an oral hearing, details of your representative, and other matters.

### Tax credits

When an appeal has been made against a tax credits decision, HM Revenue and Customs often wants to 'settle' the appeal before it is considered by the tribunal. This can only happen with your consent.

If the appeal is settled, then it 'lapses' (it does not go ahead). So think carefully about whether or not to settle the appeal.

If you agree to settle, the terms of the agreement must be set in a written notice.

The appeal then lapses unless you write back within 30 days of the date of the written notice saying that you have changed your mind and want the appeal to go ahead. If the appeal is not settled, HM Revenue and Customs prepares its response to the appeal and sends it out in the appeal papers to HM Courts and Tribunals Service and to you. HM Courts and Tribunals Service then takes over the handling of the appeal, and sends you an enquiry form asking about your availability, whether you want an oral hearing, details of your representative, and other matters.

### What if the decision maker delays?

In the past, there have sometimes been long delays in the decision maker's referring the appeal to HM Courts and Tribunals Service or in responding to the appeal. The DWP says that in appeals about universal credit or personal independence payment, it will issue its response within 28 days, and that this will apply to other benefits from October 2014.

If there is a delay by the decision maker, you can ask HM Courts and Tribunals Service to contact her/him and require that action is taken. The tribunal can issue a direction to the decision maker requiring her/him to provide documents, information or evidence, or can set a date for the hearing. The tribunal is more likely to issue a direction if you can show that the delay is causing particular problems – for example, because of your reduced income, a risk of homelessness or the interests of a child or other vulnerable person being adversely affected.

## What sorts of hearing are there?

HM Courts and Tribunals Service normally arranges for an 'oral hearing' of your appeal. This is one to which you and your representative are invited, and ideally which you should both attend. The other parties to the appeal, such as the DWP or the local authority, also have the right to attend the hearing. It is possible for there to be an oral hearing which your representative attends but you do not. However, that is not advisable, as the main value of an oral hearing is that the tribunal can ask you questions.

Having an oral hearing is strongly advisable. Only at an oral hearing can the tribunal ask you questions and find out more about things like what you can and cannot do and what happened at the medical. You are much more likely to win the appeal if there is an oral hearing.

Your appeal is dealt with at an oral hearing unless all the parties to the appeal agree to the case being dealt with at a paper hearing and the tribunal agrees it can decide the case in this way.

If there is no oral hearing, the tribunal considers your appeal just using the appeal papers – this is sometimes called a 'paper hearing' although actually there is not a hearing at all. The parties to the appeal do not have the right to attend, and no notice is sent of the date. The tribunal considers the submissions and evidence in the appeal papers. You should be given time to submit any more evidence that you may have. You do not attend a paper hearing, but remember that the chances of winning the appeal are significantly lower than at an oral hearing.

In exceptional cases, an oral hearing can take place in your home: this is called a **'domiciliary hearing'**. This can be arranged if HM Courts and Tribunals Service accepts that because of severe disability, you cannot get to a tribunal venue. If you request a domiciliary hearing, you should send a letter from a doctor confirming you are unable to travel, including by taxi. Your request may not be accepted.

If you have said that you will attend an oral hearing but at the last minute find that you cannot or that you will be late, try to let the tribunal clerk know as soon as possible.

### What happens if your representative is unavailable?

It is always advisable for both you and your representative to attend an oral hearing.

Your representative should do as much as s/he reasonably can to be available for an oral hearing if s/he wishes to attend. In general, the appeal can proceed without your representative, especially if there is no explanation about why s/he cannot attend. However, the tribunal still needs to ensure that you, as the claimant, get a fair hearing, and it should take your desire to be represented seriously. So a tribunal may grant a 'postponement' or (on the day of the hearing) an 'adjournment' of a hearing because your representative is unavailable. But the tribunal does not have to do this: it depends on the facts of the case.

If your representative cannot attend, the tribunal may expect her/his advice centre to arrange for another representative to attend. If a particular date is not suitable, it is important for her/him to explain as early as possible why this is, including, for example, why another representative cannot be there.

If your representative becomes unavailable at the last minute, a postponement can be requested – but there is no absolute requirement on the tribunal to grant this.

## What if no representative can attend the hearing?

Sometimes it is not possible for a representative to attend a hearing, wherever or whenever it is to be held. This may be the case, for example, because of limited resources in the advice centre. However, your representative can still do all the work for preparing an appeal, and in particular still send in a written 'submission' to the tribunal on your behalf.

---

Box A

**Attending an appeal without your representative**

- A written 'submission' should be prepared by your representative and sent to the tribunal in advance. This is particularly important as it is the only statement by your representative of your case. The submission should state clearly that a representative will not be attending the oral hearing, but that you will.

- Any particular difficulties you are likely to encounter during the course of the hearing (for example, because of nervousness or embarrassment) could be pointed out in the written submission.

- Your representative should give you a copy of the submission to take along to the hearing.

- You can be accompanied by someone, such as a friend or a relative, for general support and reassurance. However, it should be made clear to the tribunal that that person is not acting as your representative.

- Discuss your case with your representative before the hearing, so that you are prepared for the questions the tribunal may ask you about things like your medical condition, abilities and disabilities.

- Make an appointment with your representative for after the hearing, to discuss what happened. Your representative can take notes in case they may be of use if you appeal further to the Upper Tribunal.

---

Even if your representative cannot attend the hearing, you should still attend so the tribunal can ask you questions. See Box A for good practice if you are attending without your representative.

## Can the appeal lapse?

Once you have appealed, the decision maker can still change the decision before the appeal is heard. If s/he does this, and the new decision is more advantageous to you (even if it still does not give you everything you have appealed for) then your appeal will lapse – ie, it will not go ahead, unless you renew your appeal. If the decision maker is thinking about changing the decision, s/he may contact you and ask if you would still want to appeal if a new decision is made. If you are contacted about this, ask your representative for advice. Unless the new decision would give you everything you have asked for in your appeal, it is usually better to say that you would still want to appeal. If a new decision is issued before the appeal is heard, and you do not want your appeal to lapse, make sure you renew your appeal. It is not very common for an appeal to lapse.

## Can the hearing be postponed or adjourned?

Once a date has been set for the hearing of the appeal, before the day of the hearing it can be 'postponed' (ie, put off) until a later date. Once hearing has started, it can be 'adjourned' (ie, paused) until another day. The tribunal does not have to postpone or adjourn the hearing, and usually will not do so unless it is absolutely necessary. If you (or your representative) apply for a postponement or adjournment, explain your reasons for the request as fully as possible.

Whether or not a hearing is postponed or adjourned depends on the facts of the case. The tribunal should bear in mind the need to deal with cases fairly and justly. But the tribunal must also deal with cases flexibly, and parties to the appeal are expected to co-operate with the running of the appeal, including as far as possible making sure that their case is ready. In general, a tribunal may adjourn for something like sudden illness, but not if you or your representative repeatedly ask for more time to produce evidence.

*What the law says*

### Postponements and adjournments

The First-tier Tribunal may adjourn or postpone a hearing. If a party fails to attend a hearing, the tribunal may proceed in her/his absence if the tribunal is satisfied s/he has been notified of the hearing and considers that it is in the interests of justice to proceed.

*Rules 5 and 31 The Tribunal Procedure (First-tier Tribunal) (Social Entitlement Chamber) Rules 2008*

In practice, a tribunal is often happy to grant a very short adjournment (such as for 10 minutes or so to enable you or your representative to collect your thoughts) but it would be very reluctant to adjourn until another day. However, it may well do so if you have new evidence or arguments on the day of the tribunal, which it thinks the other party to the appeal must be given time to consider.

If a postponement or adjournment is refused, the hearing goes ahead and you and your representative must be prepared to continue. If a postponement is refused, you can still request an adjournment on the day of the hearing, but again if refused, the hearing will take place.

*What the law says*

### Adjourning an appeal

The likely approach of a tribunal to a request for adjournment would focus on: (1) what would be the benefit of an adjournment, (2) why was the party not ready to proceed; and (3) what impact would an adjournment have on the other party and the operation of the tribunal system?

*MA v Secretary of State for Work and Pensions [2009] UKUT 211 (AAC) (a decision of the Upper Tribunal)*

## Can the appeal be withdrawn?

If you 'withdraw' your appeal, that means it is not considered by the tribunal, and the original decision that you appealed against stands.

You can withdraw your appeal at any time before the tribunal makes its decision. You do not have to give reasons for withdrawing your appeal, but in some cases the tribunal's permission is required.

Once the tribunal has started the hearing, or in any case where the tribunal has directed that its permission is required, the appeal can only be withdrawn with the tribunal's permission (in which case you may have to give your reasons).

You must apply to withdraw an appeal in writing if the hearing has not yet started, but once it has started, your application can be made orally. In practice, HM Courts and Tribunals Service may be willing to ignore (or 'waive') the requirement that the application is in writing, and accept notification by telephone.

If your appeal has been withdrawn, it can be reinstated by the tribunal. For this to happen, you must apply to the tribunal in writing. Your application must be received within one month of the date the tribunal received the application to withdraw.

## Can the appeal be cancelled?

An appeal can be cancelled (known as 'struck out') by the tribunal in the following circumstances.

- You have not complied with a direction from the tribunal – for example, you have not supplied information it has required. Your appeal is cancelled automatically if the direction stated that failure to comply would lead to a strike out. Make sure that you always respond promptly.

- The tribunal does not have jurisdiction to deal with the appeal – for example, because there is no right of appeal against the decision. You must be given a chance to comment before your appeal is cancelled.

- The tribunal considers that the appeal has no realistic prospect of success. You must be given a chance to comment before your appeal is cancelled.

- You have failed to co-operate with the tribunal to the extent that the case cannot be dealt with fairly or justly. You must be given a chance to comment first.

If your appeal is cancelled for failure to comply with a direction from the tribunal, you can apply for the appeal to be reinstated. You must apply in writing, and your application must be received within a month of the date the strike out was sent, although longer may be allowed. Your application should be accompanied by the reasons why the direction could not reasonably be complied with.

In other cases reinstatement is not possible, but before your appeal is cancelled you should first be given a chance to comment and say why the appeal should not be struck out – for example, why there was good reason for failing to co-operate with the tribunal.

Decisions to strike out an appeal or to refuse to reinstate a struck-out appeal may be appealed further to the Upper Tribunal.

**How do you prepare for the hearing?**

An oral hearing of the appeal should be requested if possible. That means a hearing that is attended by you and ideally your representative. You and your representative should discuss your case before the hearing. You should both be clear about what you consider to be the relevant facts, and what your case will be.

You should be prepared for the tribunal to ask you questions at the hearing about the relevant facts in your case. This is the most important part of the oral hearing. Being prepared for questioning means understanding that the tribunal will ask you direct questions about relevant facts. It does not mean that you should give prepared answers or behave in a particular way. You should respond to the tribunal's questions as honestly and as accurately as you can. Try neither to exaggerate nor to underestimate things when giving your answers, and be as clear as you can.

**What questions might the tribunal ask?**

The tribunal asks you about the relevant facts in your case. For example, you may be asked questions about things like how far you can walk, whether you can concentrate on a magazine or television programme or what happened at your medical. Depending on the facts of your case, some of the questions may be quite personal – for example, about your medical condition and how it affects your daily life.

In appeals about the work capability assessment, personal independence payment or disability living allowance, one of the members of the tribunal will be medically qualified and will probably ask questions about your treatment and medication.

You will not be asked questions about the law, but your representative may be asked whether s/he has relied on a particular rule or piece of caselaw. However, most oral hearings do not involve long debates about the law.

In some cases, where there is someone present representing the decision maker (a 'presenting officer'), s/he may be permitted to ask you some questions. S/he can only ask you about relevant facts in the case and cannot ask you questions about the law.

The tribunal can observe your behaviour – for example when you walk into the room and how comfortably you sit during the hearing – and draw conclusions from that. However, the tribunal cannot conduct a medical examination, except in appeals about industrial injuries disablement benefit.

**Will the tribunal question a child, a vulnerable adult or sensitive witness?**

The tribunal will not usually question a child, even where the child is the claimant (such as where disability living allowance has been claimed for her/him). Similarly, the tribunal does not usually question a vulnerable adult or sensitive witness.

*What the law says*

## Questioning children, vulnerable adults or sensitive witnesses

The tribunal will only ask a child, vulnerable adult or sensitive witness questions where it considers it necessary for a fair hearing and that the person's welfare is not prejudiced. In deciding what to do, the tribunal should have regard to all the available evidence and, for example, what the child's parent or carer (or their representative) says.

*Practice Direction (First-tier and Upper Tribunals): Child, Vulnerable Adult and Sensitive Witnesses), Senior President of Tribunals, 30 October 2008*

Tell the tribunal in advance if you do not want your child to be at the hearing and be questioned.

Box B
### Final preparations for the hearing

- Check that you (or your representative) have your appeal papers and a copy of your submission to bring to the hearing.

- Remember that the tribunal will ask you questions in the hearing.

- Plan to arrive in good time at the tribunal venue.

- Neither you nor your representative are required to wear formal dress for the hearing, although your representative may wish, for example, to wear a suit. You should ensure that you feel comfortable.

Box C
### Checklist for representatives

Your representative should do the following.

- Check that both of you are familiar with the submission. It will damage your chances of winning your appeal if you say different things at the appeal hearing.

- Ensure that your submission has been sent in to the tribunal in advance (submitting it on the day may cause an adjournment), with any further evidence and the letters asking for such evidence. Your representative should bring spare copies of these documents to the hearing.

- Think about the sort of questions the tribunal may ask you and ensure that you understand that s/he usually cannot answer for you.

- Make any witnesses aware of what the tribunal will be like and the sort of questions that may be asked.

- Have the appeal papers and copies of any legislation that are particularly relevant.

- Bring writing materials to make notes.

## 2. What happens at the hearing?

Oral hearings take place on the date and time and at the place notified (unless there has been a postponement). Hearings normally take place between 10am and 12.45pm and 2pm and 4.45pm. Some appeals may be on Saturdays.

### What happens when you arrive?

When you arrive at the tribunal venue, you wait in a waiting room and eventually you are met by the clerk to the tribunal. The clerk asks you whether you have any expenses for attending the appeal such as travel expenses or loss of earnings. Your representative is not able to claim expenses. The clerk will also ask whether you have any further evidence that you want to submit, and whether you have any witnesses.

If you do not have a representative, the clerk may give you a brief outline of what is likely to happen in the hearing. If you have any questions about that, ask the clerk.

Depending on the venue, there may be other people in the waiting room. Usually these will be other claimants and their representatives, as the tribunal hears a number of cases each day. A 'presenting officer' may also be in the waiting room.

When the tribunal is ready to start, the clerk asks all parties to the appeal into the tribunal room. If there is a witness, s/he may be asked to wait outside the tribunal room, and only be called in when the tribunal is ready to ask her/him questions.

## Who is a presenting officer?

Sometimes, there may be someone from the body that made the decision under appeal, such as the Department for Work and Pensions (DWP). This person is called a 'presenting officer' and is there to explain the decision. A presenting officer is a party to the appeal and can make submissions and ask questions. Her/his role is supposed to be that of a 'friend of the court', that is to help the tribunal make its decision, rather than defend the decision under appeal at all costs. The presenting officer may be in the waiting room or in a waiting room of her/his own. The presenting officer should not be in the tribunal room until the hearing starts. In recent years, it has become increasingly common for presenting officers not to attend hearings. The presenting officer can ask you questions, although it is relatively uncommon. The presenting officer should not attempt to cross examine you as if you were a witness or defendant in a criminal trial; rather, s/he should do so to help the tribunal make its decision.

## What is the tribunal room like?

Tribunal rooms may differ slightly from venue to venue, but in most cases the tribunal members are seated on one side of a large table. They usually sit on normal chairs, not on a raised platform. The judge sits in the middle, with the other members of the tribunal (if present) alongside.

The tribunal has copies of the appeal papers and the legislation, including the *Social Security Legislation* volumes, published by Sweet and Maxwell. The clerk to the tribunal is there to assist with other information and administrative matters.

The parties to the appeal and their representatives are invited to sit on the other side of the table. You are normally asked to sit in the middle (opposite the judge), with your representative to one side and the presenting officer (if present) to the other. The clerk to the tribunal sits on an adjoining side of the table, but often leaves and re-enters the room during the course of the hearing. The clerk may be working at a computer during the hearing.

**Who are the members of the tribunal?**

Tribunals consist of one, two or three members, depending on the type of decision that is being appealed. There is more information on this in Chapter 2.

The tribunal members do not wear judicial wigs or gowns. They are, however, likely to be dressed relatively formally, wearing suits or other smart dress. They usually refer to themselves (and can be addressed) as 'Mr', 'Mrs' or 'Ms', although there are no rules about such things. Some judges refer to themselves as 'Judge'.

**Who else may be present?**

Usually, there is no one else in the room apart from the members of the tribunal, the parties to the appeal (you, your representative and, if present, the presenting officer) and the clerk.

Sometimes, someone undergoing training with HM Courts and Tribunals Service may be present to observe the hearing. S/he sits to the side or at the back of the room.

Witnesses may be present if they have been called by a party to the appeal or under a direction from the tribunal. In many appeals there are no witnesses. If there are witnesses, the tribunal will probably direct that they are present in the tribunal room only for questioning.

In theory, hearings are heard in public and any member of the public may also be present. In practice, it is almost unheard of for this to happen. If you want to protect your privacy, you can ask the tribunal to exclude members of the public.

*What the law says*

> **Tribunal hearings**
>
> Hearings are to be in public, but a tribunal may direct that a hearing, or part of it, is held in private and may exclude a person from a hearing.
>
> *Rule 30 The Tribunal Procedure (First-tier Tribunal) (Social Entitlement Chamber) Rules 2008*

## What happens at the hearing?

There are no set rules on exactly how a tribunal must be run or the order in which things must happen. Instead, there are rules that give the tribunal wide discretion to decide what happens. The main requirement is that the hearing is fair – that all parties are given a chance to put their case, and that there is no bias.

The judge usually decides exactly what happens and in what order. This includes deciding (if necessary) that a part of the hearing should be in private. It also includes giving a direction to a party to the appeal – for example, to produce a particular piece of evidence. For instance, the DWP can be directed to produce a medical report.

*What the law says*

> **Tribunal hearings**
>
> The tribunal may 'regulate its own procedure' and 'give a direction in relation to the conduct or disposal of proceedings at any time'.
>
> *Rule 5 The Tribunal Procedure (First-tier Tribunal) (Social Entitlement Chamber) Rules 2008*

## How does the hearing begin?

First the judge introduces the tribunal to you. If your hearing is being recorded on tape, the judge explains that and asks everyone present (except the clerk) to introduce themselves for the tape.

The judge explains what the tribunal is and what its job is, as well as introducing any other members of the tribunal. The judge normally emphasises the independence of the tribunal.

Usually the judge summarises what is at issue in the appeal and may invite the parties to the appeal to outline their case, although s/he could, for example, move straight on to evidence and questions.

This means the judge may turn to your representative quite early in the proceedings and ask her/him to outline the decision you are seeking, or if there is anything to add to your written submission.

During the hearing, the judge makes notes – known as a 'record of proceedings'. They are not part of the decision but can be requested after the hearing.

## What happens after the introductions?

Usually after the case has been outlined, the tribunal begins asking questions. The judge and the other members of the tribunal (if present) may all ask questions.

The main aim is to get oral evidence from you. Usually, that means questions about factual matters such as about your medical condition and treatment and your abilities and disabilities. The tribunal will not question you about the law. The tribunal may ask you some sensitive or embarrassing questions, but this is often necessary in order to get the evidence that is required.

The tribunal does not want your representative to give answers for you. It may ask your representative some questions about the written submission, but often says relatively little to your representative.

Although the tribunal members usually try to be friendly, questioning can sometimes appear abrupt. This is usually because the tribunal is conscious of time and the need to be able to deal with other cases on the same day. If you become upset or confused by the questioning, indicate this to the judge and ask if it is possible to slow down, or to rephrase the question. Your representative can ask for this on your behalf. If you become very upset, the tribunal may allow a short adjournment. Exceptionally, the tribunal may allow your representative to speak for you if it accepts that you cannot.

The tribunal usually asks the parties to the appeal if they want to ask any questions. This may be the point at which your representative wants to ask you a question, to clarify or emphasise a point that s/he thinks is important and has perhaps been misunderstood or ignored. The presenting officer, if present, may also ask questions. After that, evidence is taken from any witnesses that are attending the hearing.

## What CPAG says

### Should your representative tell you exactly what answers to give?

You should answer questions in your own words and always be truthful. Your representative should prepare you for the sort of questions you may be asked and the general way in which you should answer. So your representative may emphasise not only the need to be truthful, but also the need to be as clear as possible about what you can and cannot do. That may mean not being unnecessarily brave about things like the pain or distress that you feel, remembering to be clear about variations in your ability, and pointing out if you have taken extra medication in order to be able to attend the hearing.

## EXAMPLES

### At the tribunal

Sofia's representative thinks that Sofia has been confused by the questions the tribunal has asked and asks the judge if she can put a question to Sofia. The judge agrees, although he asks her representative to wait until the tribunal has finished asking its questions.

Maggie becomes upset during the hearing. Her representative indicates this to the judge and respectfully asks whether the tribunal could put the questions in another way.

Fred's representative wants to give a lot of details about Fred's appeal at the start of the hearing. The judge asks the representative just to outline the basis of the appeal, and explains that the tribunal will ask Fred some questions. The representative is given a chance to make any other comments before the hearing ends.

### Is there a medical examination?

The tribunal does not conduct a medical examination, except in industrial injuries benefit cases. In an industrial injuries benefit appeal, there is usually a pause in the proceedings and you are taken into an examination room to be examined by the medical member of the tribunal.

However, although the tribunal cannot conduct a medical examination, it is entitled to observe how you behave, such as your walking ability when you enter the tribunal room or your ability to remain comfortable in the tribunal, and use those observations as evidence.

### Can the tribunal make a less favourable decision?

The tribunal can make a decision that is actually less favourable to you than the one which you are appealing against. This usually happens where there is a part of a decision that you are happy with and do not want to be changed. It can occur particularly, but not exclusively, in appeals about personal independence payment or disability living allowance. For more information, see Chapter 5.

**EXAMPLE**

**Less favourable decision**

Ade has appealed against the refusal to award him the daily living component of personal independence payment. He was awarded the mobility component at the standard rate, and he is happy with that.

However, although he has only asked the tribunal to look at the daily living component, the tribunal thinks that the award of the mobility component is incorrect, and warns Ade that it will consider removing that. It gives him a chance to consider what he wants to do next (for example, request an adjournment or withdraw his appeal).

## How does the hearing end?

When all the evidence has been heard by the tribunal, the judge usually asks whether there are any 'closing statements'. This is your or your representative's chance to briefly sum up the case, drawing attention to particular strong points and emphasising any particular points that have come up in the course of the hearing.

After the closing statements, the parties to the appeal and their representatives are asked to leave the tribunal room while the tribunal makes its decision.

In most cases, a decision is made and given to you on the day. There is no requirement on the tribunal to do so. If the judge thinks that a decision cannot be made on the day and needs to be sent in writing later, s/he will say so.

When the tribunal has made its decision, you are invited back into the tribunal room to be informed of the decision. Sometimes, the tribunal may invite only your representative back into the room, as tribunals often prefer to deal with the representative at this stage. However, if you wish also to be present, that should normally be allowed.

The decision is given verbally by the judge, along with a short written summary of the decision, called the 'decision notice'. This is the formal end to the hearing. It is not a further opportunity to make points or ask questions.

## 3. What happens after the decision is made?

When you have left the tribunal room after getting the decision notice, make sure that you understand the decision and what it means for your benefit or tax credit entitlement, and that it is consistent with what you understood the tribunal said the decision would be. Check this with your representative if necessary.

If a presenting officer was at the hearing, s/he normally makes sure that the organisation that made the original decision, for instance the Department for Work and Pensions (DWP), gets the decision notice. If not, the clerk ensures that it is sent.

### Did you win your appeal?

If you win your appeal, usually the decision refusing you benefit is usually replaced with one awarding benefit.

Although the tribunal decision is binding, the decision maker is responsible for implementing it, not the tribunal. Sometimes the decision maker may need to make further decisions about your entitlement – for example, when the tribunal has held that you have a right to reside, and your income and capital then need to be assessed. The tribunal has no legal power to enforce payment.

In rare cases, the decision maker may want to make a further appeal to the Upper Tribunal against the decision of the tribunal. If this happens, payment of your benefit following the appeal is suspended (not actually paid). However, a further appeal is considered only where an important point of general legal principle is at issue. In the vast majority of cases, the decision maker does not appeal further.

### Can you be paid arrears?

If you win your appeal, you may be entitled not only to benefit from now on, but also to arrears of benefit that was not paid while the appeal was pending.

Sometimes, arrears are reduced by the amount of another, 'overlapping' benefit that was paid to you while you were waiting for the appeal to be decided. An overlapping benefit is one that cannot be paid at the same time as another. For example, if you were paid jobseeker's allowance while waiting for your appeal about employment and support allowance to be decided, the two benefits will have overlapped and the arrears of your employment and support allowance are reduced by the jobseeker's allowance you have received. Generally speaking, arrears of personal independence payment or disability living allowance are not reduced.

Arrears of benefit may count as your capital for the purpose of means-tested benefits like universal credit or income support. The general rule is that arrears of benefit are ignored for 52 weeks after they are received. But arrears of some benefits are always ignored. These include attendance allowance, disability living allowance, personal independence payment and income-related employment and support allowance (but not contributory employment and support allowance).

Box D

**Q&A: winning an appeal**

**Q.** Lenka's appeal was about the work capability assessment. Does winning mean that she will always have limited capability for work?
**A.** No. Generally speaking, the DWP is still able to arrange further medicals to assess her limited capability for work in the future. The tribunal may have made a recommendation about how long it should be before she is reassessed. But the DWP does not have to follow that. The same applies to decisions about the tests for entitlement to personal independence payment or disability living allowance.

**Q.** Archie wins his appeal. When will he start getting his money?

**A.** There is no set period. In most cases, benefit starts to be paid again within a few weeks of the tribunal decision. If there is a delay, contact the decision maker and ask that payment begins as soon as possible. Note that the decision maker has at least a month in which to ask for a statement of reasons for the tribunal's decision (for more on this, see Chapter 7).

### Did you lose your appeal?

If lose your appeal, there are a number of options. Ask your representative or an advice centre about these.

- Consider whether the decision could be 'set aside', or whether you can make a further appeal to the Upper Tribunal. There is more information about this in Chapter 7.

- If the tribunal awarded you some benefit, though not everything you asked for, and you have had a change of circumstances since the tribunal decision, consider requesting the decision maker to look at the decision again and make a new decision on your entitlement, called a 'supersession'. This is a decision that changes the decision that the tribunal made. Note that, generally, even if the supersession increases your award, you do not get any arrears.

- Accept the decision and if possible reclaim, or make a claim for a different benefit.

Box E
**Q&A: losing an appeal**

**Q.** Sasha was paid employment and support allowance while waiting for her appeal to be decided. Must she pay that employment and support allowance back?
**A.** No. The decision maker only removes entitlement from the date of the tribunal's decision, and Sasha remains entitled to the employment and support allowance that she was paid – though that award stops now.

**Q.** Teresa lost her appeal about failure of the work capability assessment. Can she try to claim employment and support allowance again?

**A.** Yes. If it is more than six months since the original decision of the decision maker, then she should be able to get employment and support allowance straight away, as long as she submits a medical certificate. A new work capability assessment will be arranged. If it is not more than six months since the original decision, she can still reclaim, but she will not get employment and support allowance again until she satisfies a new work capability assessment.

**Q.** Sean lost his appeal about entitlement to personal independence payment. Can he reapply?

**A.** Yes, Sean can reapply. Any entitlement he has only starts from the date of his new claim. In practice, the decision maker may look to see whether there has been any change of circumstance that means that s/he should not just make the same decision as was made previously. But there is nothing to prevent a repeat claim.

**Q.** Liam lost his appeal about being entitled to tax credits as a single person because he was held to be part of a couple. This means that he has been overpaid. Can he appeal if HM Revenue and Customs decides to recover the overpayment?

**A.** No. A decision to recover an overpayment of tax credit cannot be appealed, although Liam can appeal against the decision that he was part of a couple. The decision to recover the overpayment can be disputed with HM Revenue and Customs. If he would have been entitled to it as a couple, he should ask for the overpayment to be reduced by the amount he would have got as a couple.

# Chapter 7
# After the appeal

**This chapter covers:**

1. How are you notified of the decision?

2. Can the tribunal decision be changed?

3. Can you make a further appeal?

4. What happens after you start a further appeal?

## What you need to know

- A summary decision notice is usually issued to you on the day of the hearing.

- You can request a statement of reasons. You should do this in particular if you lost your appeal and may want to make a further appeal.

- The tribunal decision is binding unless it is changed (for example, due to it being set aside) or changed on further appeal to the Upper Tribunal.

- You can make a further appeal to the Upper Tribunal, but only on the basis of an error of law in the tribunal decision, not simply because you disagree with it.

## 1. How are you notified of the decision?

When the tribunal has made its decision, a short written summary of the decision (a 'decision notice') is usually handed out on the day of your hearing. More rarely, the tribunal posts the decision notice to you at a later date.

The decision notice should include your right to request a statement of reasons for the decision, and the conditions for making a further appeal to the Upper Tribunal.

*What the law says*

### Tribunal decisions

A decision notice must be provided as soon as reasonably practicable.

A written statement of reasons must be supplied, if requested, within one month of the date on which the decision was given.

*Rules 33 and 34 The Tribunal Procedure (First-tier Tribunal) (Social Entitlement Chamber) Rules 2008*

## Statement of reasons

The 'statement of reasons' is longer than the decision notice, and includes the findings of fact made by the tribunal, and a full explanation of why the tribunal made its decision. For example, it should include an explanation of the evidence the tribunal preferred (if any) and why it preferred it. (Sometimes the statement of reasons may also be referred to as the 'full written decision' or 'written reasons'.)

It is important to have a statement of reasons if you are considering an appeal to the Upper Tribunal. It is often difficult to show that there is an error of law in the tribunal's decision if there is no statement of reasons. Without an error of law in the decision, there can be no further appeal to the Upper Tribunal.

Sometimes the tribunal provides a written statement of reasons for the decision automatically. If not, you can request a statement of reasons from the tribunal.

A request for a statement of reasons must be in writing. There is a time limit. If the request is received by the First-tier Tribunal within one month of the decision notice being given (or sent), the tribunal *must* provide one. If the request Is outside the one-month time limit, the tribunal can still provide one but does not have to. If the request is late, explain why.

The tribunal should send a statement of reasons within a month of your request 'or as soon as is reasonably practicable' after that period.

The time limit for appealing to the Upper Tribunal does not start until the statement of reasons is sent. If there is a long delay, contact HM Courts and Tribunals Service and ask what the reason for the delay is, and that the statement of reasons be sent as soon as possible.

**Record of proceedings**

The judge makes a written note of the things that happened in the hearing, called a 'record of proceedings'. It should include things like the evidence taken and any requests for an adjournment that were made and the response given. Sometimes, your oral hearing may have been recorded on tape.

The record of proceedings is not a formal part of the tribunal's decision. It is not usually sent out as a matter of course, even where a statement of reasons is requested. It is not essential to have a record of proceedings to appeal against a tribunal decision. However, it is sometimes a good idea to request the record of proceedings if a statement of reasons is requested, as it can provide more background to the decision and help identify any errors of law. If you do request a record of proceedings, it is a good idea to do this in the same letter in which you ask for a statement of reasons.

Applications for a record of proceedings must be made in writing within six months of the date of the tribunal's decision. The tribunal may still supply one if the request is made after the end of that time limit, but does not have to, and records of proceedings may be destroyed after six months. There is no absolute requirement to provide a record of proceedings even if requested, although a failure to provide one requested within the time limit may suggest that the decision is not as well-founded as it should be.

## 2. Can the tribunal decision be changed?

The tribunal decision can be changed, but only if certain conditions are met. Unless it is changed, your tribunal decision is binding.

If you want the tribunal decision to be changed, it is strongly advisable to get advice about this from your representative or an advice centre.

Any party to the appeal can try to change a tribunal decision in the ways set out below. For example, the decision maker, as well as you, can try to appeal further to the Upper Tribunal. In practice, however, the decision maker usually only tries to appeal to the Upper Tribunal when a general point of legal principle is involved.

There are a number of ways a tribunal decision can be changed.

- A **clerical mistake or other accidental slip or omission** can be corrected by the tribunal itself. This is to allow decisions to be altered very quickly for simple clerical mistakes and 'slips of the pen'.

- In certain circumstances, it can be **'set aside'** (cancelled) and the appeal heard again.

- If there is an error of law in the tribunal decision, it can be appealed further to the **Upper Tribunal**. (If this is applied for and there is a clear error of law, the tribunal can review its own decision before it is reconsidered by the Upper Tribunal, in which case you should be notified of your right to appeal against that.)

- If the decision includes an award of benefit, it can be looked again by the decision maker if there are grounds to do so. This is called a **'supersession'**. Usually, this happens if there has been a relevant change in your circumstances since the date of the decision – for example, where your condition changed while you were waiting for your appeal to be heard. (A supersession cannot be carried out just because the decision maker thinks the decision is legally wrong – in that case, s/he must try to make an appeal to the Upper Tribunal.)

## When can the decision be set aside?

*What the law says*

### Clerical mistakes and set asides

The tribunal may at any time correct any clerical mistake or other accidental slip or omission in a decision.

The tribunal may set aside a decision which disposes of proceedings and remake the decision.

*Rules 36 and 37 The Tribunal Procedure (First-tier Tribunal) (Social Entitlement Chamber) Rules 2008*

A tribunal decision can only be 'set aside' in certain circumstances. The main purpose of the rule is to allow speedy cancellations of decisions where something went wrong with the procedure of the tribunal. Examples include where you or your representative were prevented from attending the oral hearing at the last minute but the tribunal went ahead anyway, or where you received relevant evidence just too late for the hearing. Much depends on the individual facts of the case. If the tribunal decision is set aside, a new tribunal decision needs to be made.

The tribunal sets a decision aside if it considers that it is 'in the interests of justice' to do so, and:

- a party to the appeal or her/his representative did not receive the appeal papers or other relevant documents in enough time for the hearing
- a party to the appeal was not present at the oral hearing (but not if s/he had chosen not to attend)
- there was some other 'procedural irregularity'

Under a separate rule, which is likely to apply only in rare cases, the tribunal's decision *must* be set aside if an application is made for permission to appeal to the Upper Tribunal, and both you *and* the decision maker agree that the tribunal made an error of law. It is rare for both parties to the appeal to agree about this. Also, normally the tribunal does not send copies of applications for permission to appeal to the other party to the appeal.

Applications to set aside must be in writing and be received by HM Courts and Tribunals Service no later than one month after the date on which the tribunal decision was sent. The rules do not refer to the situation where the decision was given at the hearing rather than sent through the post, but in practice are applied as meaning within one month of the date of the hearing. The tribunal can allow longer than one month but it does not have to. If the request is late, explain why. When you ask for a set aside, you can also ask that if the request is refused, then you be sent a statement of reasons (as you may then want to consider whether there are grounds for a further appeal to the Upper Tribunal).

If the decision is set aside, the appeal must be heard again. If the decision is not set aside, the tribunal can treat the application as one for permission to appeal to the Upper Tribunal or as an application for correction of the decision.

A refusal to set aside can be the subject of an appeal to the Upper Tribunal. Sometimes, the reason for a set aside may also be an error of law and so also potentially the subject of an appeal to the Upper Tribunal. For example, if relevant evidence was not included in the appeal papers, then depending on the facts of the case, that is potentially both a ground for a set aside and an error of law in that it was a breach of the rules of natural justice. In such cases, it may be worth trying to appeal to the Upper Tribunal both about the refusal to set aside and against the tribunal decision itself.

## 3. Can you make a further appeal?

If there is an error of law in the First-tier Tribunal decision, there is a right of further appeal to the Upper Tribunal. All parties to the appeal have the right of further appeal. Only a few decisions (called 'excluded' decisions) do not have the right to a further appeal.

**What the law says**

## Appealing to the Upper Tribunal

There is a right of appeal to the Upper Tribunal on any point of law arising from a decision made by the First-tier Tribunal other than an excluded decision.

*Section 11 Tribunals, Courts and Enforcement Act 2007*

There is a one-month time limit for applying (although this can be extended). There is a right of further appeal against most tribunal decisions, including not only final decisions of the tribunal, but also things like decisions on whether to admit a late appeal.

Box A
### Appeals to the Upper Tribunal

- Appeals to the Upper Tribunal can only be on the basis of an 'error of law'.

- Upper Tribunal appeals are more legalistic and can seem more formal than First-tier Tribunals. For example, if there is an oral hearing (which is relatively rare) the decision maker is represented by a lawyer. However, unnecessary formality is supposed to be avoided.

- All parties to the appeal have the right of further appeal.

- It is advisable to have the statement of reasons for the tribunal's decision before trying to appeal to the Upper Tribunal.

- Permission to appeal has to be applied for, and the application must initially be made to the First-tier Tribunal, within the time limit.

- Decisions of the Upper Tribunal are binding caselaw on all decision makers and First-tier Tribunals, so its decisions affect all claimants, not just those in the individual case.

If the decision maker intends to make a further appeal and gives you written notice of that, payment of your benefit awarded under the tribunal decision can be suspended.

The further appeal is made to the Upper Tribunal. This guide is not intended as a guide to such appeals. Here, we just set out some of the basic rules and explain how to get an appeal to the Upper Tribunal started.

As the Upper Tribunal is only concerned with matters of law, it is generally much less concerned with matters of fact and evidence. This means that appeals to the Upper Tribunal are more legalistic and can seem more formal. The judges who sit on the Upper Tribunal are experts in social security law. The submissions made for the decision maker are drawn up by lawyers. However, the Upper Tribunal has procedural rules that in many respects are similar to those that apply to First-tier Tribunals. In particular, the 'overriding objective' is to deal with cases 'fairly and justly', which includes avoiding unnecessary formality. Parties should be able to participate fully in the proceedings, and have the right to appoint a representative, who need not be legally qualified.

## Do you need a representative?

There is no requirement that you have a representative for an appeal to the Upper Tribunal, but it is strongly advisable to get help from a representative if you can. The decision maker is represented by a legally qualified person.

*What CPAG says*

### Representatives and Upper Tribunal appeals

Appeals to the Upper Tribunal are much more concerned with legal argument than most appeals to the First-tier Tribunal, and sometimes the legal argument can be complex. If you are not experienced in dealing with social security law, it is advisable to find a representative or at least seek detailed advice.

## Which decisions are excluded?

'Excluded decisions' cannot be appealed to the Upper Tribunal. These are mainly decisions the First-tier Tribunal makes about reviewing an earlier decision it made. So there is no right of appeal against a tribunal decision to review, or not to review an earlier decision, or to set aside an earlier decision on review. Also, there is no right of appeal against a decision of a First-tier Tribunal to refer a matter to the Upper Tribunal.

In these cases, an application for a 'judicial review' of the decision can be made to the Upper Tribunal.

## What is an error of law?

There is no strict definition of what is an 'error of law' in a tribunal decision. It is really a matter of judgement, taking into account the precise wording of the decision and the statement of reasons, and applying some general principles to that.

The mere fact that you disagree with the decision, or that someone else could have come to a different decision on the same facts, is not in itself an error of law.

The most common errors of law in First-tier Tribunal decisions are listed in Box B.

---

Box B
**Common errors of law in First-tier Tribunal decisions**

- The tribunal gave inadequate reasons for its decision. The tribunal's reasons should enable you to see why it reached the decision it did. Sometimes, the reason for the decision may be obvious and the tribunal does not need to spell everything out. A decision is not wrong just because evidence produced later contradicts it. But if the tribunal relied on a particular piece of evidence, or preferred one piece of evidence over another, it should say why.

- The tribunal made inadequate findings of fact for its decision, or the facts it found are such that it could not reasonably and

---

correctly have made the decision that it did. The tribunal must establish sufficient facts to support its decision. If facts are disputed, the tribunal should say which version it prefers and why.

- The tribunal applied the law incorrectly. For example, it misapplied the wording in a descriptor in the work capability assessment or in the test for personal independence payment, or took the wrong approach to deciding whether a tenancy was a 'contrived' tenancy under the housing benefit rules.

Other errors of law are possible, although in practice are less common. They are that the tribunal:

- 'breached the rules of natural justice' – see Box C
- failed to provide a statement of reasons for its decision where it had a duty to do so
- took things into account which it should not have, or refused to take into account things which it should have
- conducted a physical examination and based its decision upon that (except industrial injuries benefits cases)

Box C
**Natural justice**

The idea of 'natural justice' is a broad one, but can be summed up as meaning that each party to the appeal must be given a fair chance to put their case. The specific requirement for a tribunal to deal with a case 'fairly and justly' is part of this. This error can be difficult to show as much depends on the facts – getting the record of proceedings may help. Examples of such errors can include where the tribunal held the oral hearing in your absence even though you intended to be there. The mere fact that you found the tribunal abrupt or unfriendly is not enough – but in any case the individual facts in your case will be very important.

> **What the law says**
>
> **Breach of natural justice**
>
> It is a breach of natural justice if the claimant through no fault of her/his own does not get notice of the hearing and so does not get the chance to put her/his case.
>
> *CDLA/5413/1999; CIB/303/1999 (decisions of the Social Security Commissioners)*

## 4. What happens after you start a further appeal?

A judge of the First-tier Tribunal considers an application for permission to appeal to the Upper Tribunal. If permission is refused, the application can be remade directly to the Upper Tribunal.

The decision maker may have applied for permission to appeal. If the decision maker applies for permission to appeal within the time limit, payment of any benefit awarded to you under the tribunal decision can continue to be suspended.

### What can the First-tier Tribunal do?

The judge who considers the application for permission to appeal to the Upper Tribunal may not be the same judge who was on the tribunal that heard your appeal. In response to the application, the judge can do any of the following.

- Grant permission to appeal. You are notified of this, and (if you have applied for permission to appeal) you must then send a 'notice of appeal' to the Upper Tribunal so that it is received within one month of your being sent the permission to appeal. You are sent Form UT1 to do this. The Upper Tribunal can extend the time limit but does not have to. If you send the notice of appeal late, explain why. You should include with the form the notice granting permission to appeal and a copy of the tribunal's decisions and statement of reasons (if you have one).

- Refuse permission to appeal. You must be notified of this in writing, along with a statement of reasons for the refusal and notice of your right to apply directly to the Upper Tribunal for permission to appeal.

- Review the First-tier Tribunal decision, but only if satisfied that there is an error of law in it. This only applies in very clear cases of error of law, and is not common.

If there is no statement of reasons for the tribunal's decision because there has been no application for one, the judge must treat your application as one for a statement of reasons, and if this is provided, then permission to appeal must be applied for again. If, however, an application for a statement of reasons was refused – for example, because it was made outside the time limit – the judge can either refuse you permission to appeal or grant it.

### Review by the First-tier Tribunal

If the tribunal decision is reviewed, you must be notified of the outcome and of any right of appeal you may have. On review, the judge can:

- correct accidental errors in the decision
- amend the reasons given for the decision (but this should not mean adding new reasons the tribunal had not previously considered)
- set aside the decision (cancel it) – the tribunal must then either make a new decision or refer it to the Upper Tribunal

Generally, there is no right of further appeal against a decision to review (or not to review) the decision of the tribunal. However, it may be that there is a right of appeal where a review results in correction of an accidental error or to amend the reasons.

If the decision is set aside and a new decision made by the First-tier Tribunal, that will carry the same right of appeal as the original decision – so that you would need to apply for a statement of reasons, and request permission to appeal.

### If permission to appeal is refused

If the judge refuses permission to appeal to the Upper Tribunal, that is not necessarily the end of the matter. You can reapply directly to the Upper Tribunal. Your application should be received by the Upper Tribunal no later than one month after the date the tribunal's refusal to grant permission was sent. The Upper Tribunal can allow a longer period, but does not have to. If your application is late, explain why.

Your application to the Upper Tribunal should ideally be on Form UT1 available from HM Courts and Tribunals Service. You do not have to use the form, but your application must be in writing, and must include your details and those of your representative if you have one and identify the First-tier Tribunal decision that the application concerns. It must also include:

- the alleged error of law in the decision
- copies of the decision and the statement of reasons (if one was sent out), and the notice of the First-tier Tribunal's refusal to grant permission to appeal
- reasons for any late application for permission to appeal, both to the First-tier Tribunal and to the Upper Tribunal

However, the Upper Tribunal can ignore any irregularities in your application. If you do not have a statement of reasons for the tribunal decision, the Upper Tribunal can still grant you permission to appeal (and ultimately allow the appeal). But it remains the case that you must show that there is an error of law in the tribunal's decision – and that is more difficult without a statement of reasons. If the tribunal fails to provide a statement of reasons where it has a duty to do so (where one was requested within the one-month time limit), that is in itself an error of law.

### The response of the Upper Tribunal

The Upper Tribunal sends you a written notice on its decision on whether to grant permission to appeal.

If permission is granted, the appeal goes ahead and the Upper Tribunal considers whether or not to allow your appeal. The Upper Tribunal can either decide there was no error of law, so that the tribunal decision stands, or allow the appeal because the decision contains an error of law. In such cases, the Upper Tribunal either decides itself what the correct decision should have been, or sets aside (cancels) the tribunal's decision and orders that a new First-tier Tribunal should reconsider the appeal.

The Upper Tribunal may hold an oral hearing of either the application for permission to appeal or, if permission is given, of the appeal itself. However, oral hearings are not held in most cases.

If you are refused permission by the Upper Tribunal, that means your appeal will not go ahead – there is no right of further appeal. It may be possible to apply to the courts for a judicial review of the refusal, although only in cases thought to have an important point of principle or practice or some other compelling reason, as the Upper Tribunal is regarded as an expert court. Otherwise, the decision of the Upper Tribunal is final. In the vast majority of cases, the refusal of the Upper Tribunal to grant permission is the final decision.

## Judicial review in the Upper Tribunal

In a few cases, there is no right of appeal to the Upper Tribunal against the tribunal's decision. These are where the tribunal has made an 'excluded decision', such as a decision to review its own decision. In such cases it may be possible to apply for a judicial review of the excluded decision and have that considered by the Upper Tribunal (in Scotland, the application must be in the first instance to the Court of Session, who may then transfer it to the Upper Tribunal).

## Appeals to the higher courts

Decisions of the Upper Tribunal can themselves be the subject of further appeals. These appeals are to the higher courts – the Court of Appeal in England and Wales and the Court of Session in Scotland. Such appeals can only be on the basis of an error of law in the decision of the Upper Tribunal, and in practice are wholly concerned with legal argument. After that, yet further appeals are possible, again on the basis of error of law, to the Supreme Court and finally to the European courts.

## Further information

There is more information about appeals to the Upper Tribunal and the courts in CPAG's *Welfare Benefits and Tax Credits Handbook.*

# Appendix 1

## Glossary of terms

**Adjourned/adjornment**
A pause in an appeal hearing – for example, to allow a party to the appeal to consider a new point or to get more evidence.

**Appointee**
Someone, usually a relative, who is authorised by the Department for Work and Pensions to claim benefit on another person's behalf if that person cannot claim for her/himself – eg, perhaps because of a learning disability.

**Clearance time**
The time it takes for an appeal to be heard and decided by the appeal tribunal.

**Couple**
A man and a woman (or two people of the same sex) living together who are married or civil partners, or who are living together as if they were married or civil partners.

**Decision maker**
The person who makes the original decision concerning entittlment to benefit, and who considers any request for the decision to be looked at again. The decision maker does not consider or decide appeals.

**Decision notice**
A short written summary of the tribunal's decision.

**Direct lodgement**
Sending the appeal directly to HM Courts and Tribunals Service, rather than to the decision maker.

**Domicilary hearing**
An oral hearing of an appeal heard in the claimant's home rather than at a tribunal venue.

**Expediting**
The process by which the clerk to the tribunal speeds up the arrangement of an appeal hearing so that it is heard earlier than it might otherwise have been.

**First-tier Tribunal**
The independent tribunal that considers appeals against decisions.

**European Economic Area**
The 28 European Union member states, plus Iceland, Norway and Liechtenstein. For benefit purposes, Switzerland is also treated as part of the European Economic Area.

**Habitually resident**
Someone who has a settled intention to stay in the UK, and who has usually been living here for a period.

**HM Courts and Tribunals Service**
The body that administers and arranges for the independent consideration of an appeal.

**Judicial review**
A way of challenging the decisions of government departments, local authorities and some tribunals against which there is no right of appeal.

**Lapses**
Where an appeal does not go ahead because the decision has been changed with the result that the new decision is more advantageous than the old one, and the claimant has not renewed the appeal.

**Limited capability for work**
A test of whether a person's ability to work is limited by a health condition.

**Limited capability for work-related activity**
A test of how severe a person's health problems are and whether her/his ability to prepare for work is limited.

**Mandatory reconsideration**
The requirement to have a decision looked at again, via a revision, by the decision maker before an appeal can be made.

**Mandatory reconsideration notice**
The letter in which the outcome of a mandatory reconsideration is sent to the claimant.

**Means-tested benefit**
A benefit that is only paid if someone's income and capital are low enough.

**Natural justice**
**Each party to the appeal must be given a fair chance to put their case.**

**Non-contributory benefit**
A benefit for which entitlement does not depend on having paid a certain amount of national insurance contributions.

**Non-means-tested benefit**
A benefit that is paid regardless of the amount of someone's income or capital.

**Official error**
An error by for example someone at the Department for Work and Pensions or a local authority with the result that the benefit decision is wrong.

**Oral hearing**
A hearing of an appeal which the parties to the appeal have been invited to attend and (where attending) are addressed by the tribunal.

**Overpayment**
An amount of benefit that is paid which is more than a person's entitlement.

**Paper 'hearing'**
A consideration of appeal without an oral hearing – ie, by the tribunal considering the appeal papers alone.

**Party to the appeal**
The person that made the appeal and the body who made the decision which is under appeal.

**Presenting officer**
A representative from the body who made the decision under appeal who attends an oral hearing to assist in the consideration of the appeal.

**Person subject to immigration control**
Someone who requires leave to enter or remain in the UK but does not have it, or who has leave to remain but is prohibited from having recourse to public funds, or has leave to remain in the UK on the basis of a sponsorship agreement.

**Postponed/postponement**
Putting off a tribunal hearing, before it has started, so that it starts on a later date.

**Record of proceedings**
The notes made of a tribunal hearing by the judge, recording submission, evidence and procedural matters such as any consideration of adjournment.

**Revision**
A statutory method that allows benefit decisions to be changed.

**Right to reside**
A social security test, mainly affecting European Economic Area nationals, which must be satisfied in order to claim certain benefits.

**Secretary of State for Work and Pensions**
The government minister with overall responsibility for the Department for Work and Pensions; formally speaking the person who makes decisons on benefits administered by the Department.

**Set aside**
The cancelling of a tribunal decision on certain grounds.

**Slips of the pen**
Minor accidental errors in a tribunal's written decision, capable of correction by the tribunal.

**Social Security and Child Support Commissioner**
The independent judicial body that formerly considered further appeals against decisions of social security and child support tribunals.

**Struck out**
An appeal that has been cancelled, on certain grounds, before it has been considered.

**Submission**
An argument or setting out of a case, put to the tribunal. A written submission sets out the case in writing.

**Supersession**
A statutory method which allows benefit decisions to be changed, usually as a result of a change in circumstances.

**Tribunal clerk**
The official responsible for administering an appeal, includng arranging the hearing and providing administrative support to the tribunal at a hearing.

**Uphold**
Where the tribunal confirms that something is correct – for example, the tribunal may uphold the decision under appeal and so refuse to change it.

**Upper Tribunal**
The independent judicial body that considers further appeals against decisions of the First-tier Tribunal.

**Waive**
Where the tribunal uses its legal discretion so that it does not insist that a prodecural rule is followed.

# Index